Human Factors in Project Management

Human Factors in Project Management

Revised Edition

Paul C. Dinsmore

amacom

American Management Association

This book is available at a special
discount when ordered in bulk quantities.
For information, contact Special Sales Department,
AMACOM, a division of American Management Association,
135 West 50th Street, New York, NY 10020.

This publication is designed to provide accurate and authoritative information in regard to the subject matter covered. It is sold with the understanding that the publisher is not engaged in rendering legal, accounting, or other professional service. If legal advice or other expert assistance is required, the services of a competent professional person should be sought.

Library of Congress Cataloging-in-Publication Data

Dinsmore, Paul C.
    Human factors in project management / Paul C. Dinsmore.—Rev.
  ed.
     p.   cm.
  Includes bibliographical references.
  ISBN 0-8144-5003-2
  1. Industrial project management. 2. Personnel management.
I. Title.
HD69.P75D57   1990
658.4'04—dc20   89-46219
                                                 CIP

Printing number

10 9 8 7 6 5 4 3 2 1

In
memory
of
John Bell Dinsmore

Contents

Foreword

Project management is an idea whose time has come. Since its emergence in the early 1960s, project management has reached a level of maturity that has earned it an honored place in the theory and practice of contemporary management. Today, project management is recognized for what it is: a management philosophy and process that contributes to the strategic management of organizations.

Projects are building blocks in the design and execution of enterprise strategies. Research and development projects, construction projects, product and process design projects, engineering projects, and a multitude of other projects are found in the modern organization. To manage a project is to manage the design, development, and implementation of resources leading to the creation of something that did not previously exist but that is needed to enable the organization to survive and grow in its future.

The use of project management in an organization sets in motion a significant change in the culture of the user. One of the more complex results of using project management is the introduction of "matrix management"—a phrase used to describe the management of the web of relationships that come about when people join the project team and are subject to the resulting multiple authority-responsibility-accountability relationships in the organization.

The way we manage people today is undergoing enormous change. The organizational hierarchy is under attack—the "command and control" model of bureaucracy is falling to an organizational form that is more horizontal than vertical. People are—as they have always been—the common denominator that makes the organization successful. The learning that we have gained in matrix management has given us valuable insight into how people will expect to be managed in the future.

Paul C. Dinsmore, a valued friend and colleague, is a notable member of the Project Management Institute. In this book he has presented a valuable, commonsense prescription for understanding and appreciating the human side of project management. He has also provided an insightful perspective on how people will be managed in the future. His contribution is without parallel in the project management literature.

David I. Cleland
Professor of Engineering Management
School of Engineering
University of Pittsburgh

Preface to the Revised Edition

This edition of *Human Factors in Project Management* features a revision of the original 1984 edition with special attention focused on the following:

- *Update.* Developments in project management technology, practice, and behavior are incorporated, and references brought up to date.
- *Reorganization.* Sequence of presentation is altered to accommodate the updated content of the book.
- *Style.* For smoother reading, some of the references are removed and additional illustrations included.
- *Feedback.* Comments from corporate clients, fellow trainers, and consultants are also included in the revised book.

The book focuses on three angles of the human side of project management. First, *concepts* are given with explanations interspersed throughout the book. *"How to"* approaches are also spelled out with recommendations on team building, conflict management, negotiating, decision making, etc. And finally, the Second Edition is laid out as a *ready reference* for project professionals, since each chapter is devoted to a specific topic as seen through behavioral glasses.

Human Factors in Project Management

Chapter 1

People Problems and People Solutions

Our problems are man-made, therefore they can
be solved by man.

John F. Kennedy

"What are the typical problems you face in managing your projects?"

This is a question I often ask while conducting international project management seminars. In a few minutes of brainstorming, the participants generate about 60 problems that plague their projects. For example: conflicts, schedule delays, differing priorities, client interference, insufficient funding, indecision, cost overruns, inadequate specifications, and poor communication.

All these problems can either be prevented or solved by applying solid project management principles. Of these managerial problems, some are more of a technical nature, others have a strong touch of human behavior, and a good number have both technical and behavioral components. I ask the participants in the seminars to classify each problem with a T for technical, a B for behavioral, or a T/B when both factors are present. Invariably the final group result

1

shows that at least 50 percent of the problems that exist on projects are either totally or partially behavioral in nature. The percentage has reached as high as 75 percent in some groups.

The response is logical, since people are the cause of everything that happens on projects. They coordinate, manage, delegate, perform, process, decide, approve, solve problems, and carry out all the activities aimed at nursing, persuading, or jolting projects along their prescribed courses. If people make mistakes, trouble pops up. If technical or managerial competence falls below par, difficulties loom. If people fail to act, follow up, make decisions, analyze, or evaluate, projects wander off course.

People are at the center of projects in all kinds of industries including defense, construction, engineering, architecture, telecommunications, electronics, and public utilities. Projects such as presidential elections or organizational changes in companies and advertising campaigns also hinge on the human factor for success. Projects are ongoing in most industries and businesses, since a project encompasses any task grouping that has fixed goals to be achieved over a finite period.

No matter what the industry or type of project, problems occur either because people (1) make them occur or (2) don't take action to prevent them from occurring. This book presents the "whys" of project problems and sets forth "how to" routes for managing projects through the human element. Two premises make up the cornerstone of this "human side" of project management:

1. People are the cause of a project's problems.
2. A project's problems can be solved only by people.

If the majority of project problems are human behavior related, then a proportional part of managerial attention should be aimed there. This raises some related questions. For instance, just who should be devoting efforts toward managing the human factor on projects? And what fields of knowledge need to be focused on in order to manage the human element in project work? An overview response to these questions follows in this chapter, and the remainder of the book gives more detailed answers (see Figure 1–1).

Project Management Basics

The human factor approach to project management requires a solid foundation. That foundation consists of the classic principles used for organizing and dimensioning project work. Chapter 2 outlines and summarizes these principles. Here are some of the highlights:

- Project management expertise can be divided into eight categories:

    1. Scope
    2. Time
    3. Money (cost)
    4. Quality
    5. Communications
    6. Human resources
    7. Contracts and supply
    8. Risk management

- Projects develop over four phases:

    1. Conceptual
    2. Planning
    3. Execution
    4. Termination

- Completion of these phases can be accelerated by using fast-tracking techniques that involve simultaneous execution of overlapping activities. Some of the instruments used in managing projects include:

Figure 1–1. Conceptual Model of Human Factors in Project Management.

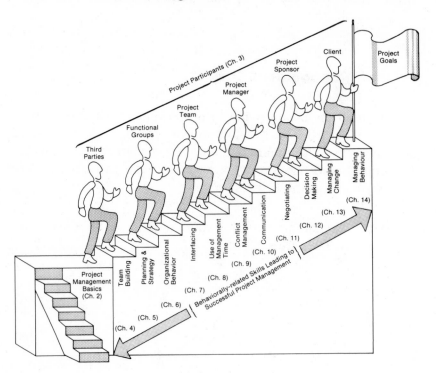

—*Work Breakdown Structure (WBS):* an analytical tool for dealing with project components in an orderly way

—*Gantt chart:* a schedule presented in bar-chart form, used for programming activities defined in the WBS

—*Cost control system:* also based on the WBS, used for detecting variations in cost estimates and for projecting future trends

—*Milestone chart:* summary of major critical activities required for completing the project

—*S-curve:* graphic technique for controlling overall project progress and productivity

—*Critical path networking:* system for calculating critical activities and for providing graphic output needed to schedule and control the project

The Players: The Project Manager and All

Just as in sports, it takes people in widely differing roles to make winning projects. Professional sports teams, whether football, basketball, baseball, or hockey, all have on-field and off-field players, including owners, managers, coaches, athletes, and support groups. Projects also have a similar cast, and all parties have to do their part for the project to meet its goals. All project players need human factor skills to make their contribution to the final effort. Here are some of the main players:

♦ Project manager
♦ Project sponsor
♦ Client
♦ Project team
♦ Functional groups
♦ Third parties

Chapter 3 describes these and other project players, with particular attention focused on the project manager. Although many project professionals possess natural capabilities and others have developed skills over the years, the entire cast of project characters needs to devote attention to improving human factor skills.

Project Blending: Building the Project Team

Getting the players to work together as a team may determine whether goals are met. Team building involves developing the capability of *people* to work together. Teamwork is both art and science. Techniques (science) help boost cooperation and productivity among team members, and yet, how those techniques are administered (art) determines their degree of effectiveness.

Here are some proven techniques that, when artfully applied, improve the effort of any project team:

- *Setting examples*—preparing the stage for role modeling and on-the-job training
- *Coaching*—including the informal chat, in-depth coaching, and using the position description as a coaching tool
- *Training sessions*—ranging from lectures and round table discussions to seminars, workshops, and formal team-building programs (see Chapter 4 for details on team building)

Planning and Strategy in Project Management

Planning is also a human factor topic, since it determines sequence and identifies who will carry out each activity. Planning, therefore, is a coordinating tool for project players to synchronize their activities. Both strategic project planning and operational plans are needed to ensure that the players carry out their respective roles. Here are the highlights of project planning:

- Plan participatively, to gain the double benefit of generating a better plan, and ensuring that it actually gets carried out.

- Recognize that individuals think differently about planning, so special efforts are called for to ensure that everyone is planning to a common base.
- Plan strategically, starting with a broad framework in the form of an overall project plan.
- Remember that only after the strategic plans determine how the project is to be managed, and how it will be carried out or built, should the detailed planning, scheduling, and controlling be addressed.

Information about planning with a human factor and strategic bias is given in Chapter 5.

Organizing Projects

Organization always involves people. Although product, geography, systems, and company culture are taken into account when organizing, the ultimate goal is to group people in such a way that work will be facilitated. Some types of organizations lend themselves to project work better than others, yet all structures are situational, and therefore, must be picked in accordance with the nature of the project and the company culture. Here are some common organizational cultures:

- *Functional:* clearly assigns responsibilities, yet tends to stimulate rigid and formal communication lines
- *Functional matrix:* introduces cross-departmental co-ordination, creating freer flowing communications and less rigid roles
- *Balanced matrix:* guarantees distinct managerial attention to both the technical and task-oriented topics, yet increases potential for organizational conflicts
- *Project matrix:* swings the matrix pendulum towards the task or mission, creating a project-oriented group supported by departments of technical expertise
- *Task force or project organization:* marshals all the human resources for the project under one command and operates relatively independently of the parent

organization, again creating a potentially conflictive situation

Chapter 6 describes the cultural and behavioral differences characteristic of each organizational structure.

Project Interfacing

Part of the interfacing necessary in project management is purely behavioral; other aspects involve the human factor to a lesser degree. Here are the main interfacing needs on projects:

- *Personal interfacing:* involving the direct interchange between people in day-to-day contacts
- *Organizational interfacing:* including the structural flow of information and communication between related project areas
- *Systems interfacing:* including physical or electronic interconnections required to make up a whole system, as well as performance criteria required for subsystems to mesh with the overall system

Interfacing can also be perceived as directional (horizontal or vertical). And it can be seen as static (permanent), or dynamic (transient). Interfacing needs and interfacing solutions change in nature over the life cycle of the project. Chapter 7 describes project interfacing in detail.

Using Managerial Time

How time is managed on projects is a determining factor for success, starting with how the project players manage their own time. Personal behavior patterns have a strong influence on how time is managed. Some of the solutions for gaining better control of time are:

- Ask yourself if you really need to see all that paper.

- Discipline your meetings for more effective results in less time.
- Determine how much time you have for one-on-one listening, problem solving, and coaching; then ration your time accordingly.

Other important principles of time management include:

- Distinguishing between subjects of true importance and those of apparent pressing urgency
- Applying Pareto's Principle to time, by using 80 percent of managerial time on 20 percent of selected subjects
- Scheduling time as opposed to scheduling work, since time is the limited resource and work must be prioritized and subordinated to available time

Chapter 8 gives results of a time management survey among project professionals, and presents recommendations on how time can best be used.

Handling Conflict

Conflict is an offspring of disagreement between individuals, and therefore is highly behavioral in nature. Conflicts may be *intrapersonal,* involving internal personal troubles, *interpersonal,* encompassing conflicts that go on between people, and *intergroup,* which pits one group against another. The causes may be "hard" (clearly defined views on two alternative administrative procedures), or "soft" (general ambiguity over role relationships in a matrix structure).

Conflict can be handled *reactively* using the five classic techniques for conflict resolution:

1. *Withdrawing*—pulling out, retreating, or giving up
2. *Smoothing*—an appeasing approach
3. *Compromising*—involving bargaining or negotiating conflicting interests

4. *Confronting*—the objective, problem-solving approach to resolving conflicts
5. *Forcing*—resorting to power or force to resolve conflict

Proactive approaches can also be used to manage conflict by using preventive situational stances with others such as subordinates, colleagues, bosses, and clients. This diminishes the probability for conflictive situations appearing in the first place.

Chapter 9 details these proactive approaches and gives other conflict management models.

Communication

Once again, people are at the center of this important factor in managing projects. The purpose of communication is to transfer information from one person or group to another. Communication depends on both effective transmittal and reception. The channel used can also have an effect on communication quality. Here are some factors that influence communications in project work:

- Communication involves conception of an idea, translation into an appropriate code or language, transmission through the right media, and monitoring of the receiver's decoding effort.
- Feedback is the quality control of communication; transmitters' and receivers' skills in stimulating and giving feedback will determine the quality of the communication.
- Types of communication used on projects include spoken, body language, written word, and graphics.
- Channels used may be face-to-face, telephone, correspondence, electronic mail, or audio visual.
- Communication flows best when good planning precedes performance.

Chapter 10 gives details on how to communicate effectively on projects.

Negotiating

Negotiating is a natural consequence of human behavior. It's a part of everyone's daily life as working relationships and terms of agreement are established. One effective approach is to negotiate on merits, which is based on four basic points:

- Separate the people from the problem.
- Focus on interests, not positions.
- Generate a variety of possibilities before deciding what to do.
- Insist that the result be based on some objective standard.

Effective negotiation is carried out in phases, starting with prenegotiation, then going on to the active negotiation, and finally moving to postnegotiation wrap up. Chapter 11 includes negotiation strategies and tactics to be used in project situations.

Decision Making and Problem Solving

Classic decision making follows a logical sequence and answers these questions:

- What constitutes the problem and its causes?
- What are the possible alternative solutions?
- What is the "best" solution?
- What is the best way to put it into effect?

Creativity is key to effective decision making and hinges on the ability of team members to interact in a positive and synergetic way.

How the decision process is conducted, in view of the nature of human behavior, also influences the effectiveness of the decision. Participative or consensus decision making is shown to boost the probability for reaching better decisions and having those decisions carried out as planned. Chapter 12 gives a detailed breakdown of the classic decision-making process and a discussion of the Japanese-style consensus.

Managing Change Across Changing Frontiers

The essence of project management is the capacity to react to and manage change. Aside from managing change throughout the duration of the project, global changes and trends in project management must also be taken into account. Here are some of the areas where change occurs:

- Primary project technology
- Communications technology
- Project management technology
- Size and nature of projects
- Organizational behavior

Change across boundaries also requires special attention as projects span cultural, technological, and national barriers. Chapter 13 presents details of managing in cross-cultural settings and reviews the challenge of technology transfer.

Human Behavior as Seen by the Experts

Experts have studied organizations for decades and devised theories as to why people behave as they do in different organizational situations. There are theories on internal and external causation, the Pygmalion Effect, and people's likes and differences. The hierarchy of human needs, the motivation-hygiene theory, and Theory X–Theory Y are popular explanations for much of the behavior in organizations. Other views include Theory Z, the expectancy theory, transactional analysis, situational leadership, the dimensional model of managerial behavior, and the Managerial Grid®. Chapter 14, "Human Behavior as Seen by the Experts," also explains yet other theories. Research in organizational be-

havior in project management settings shows findings peculiar to that area. Here are some of them, also related in
Chapter 14:

- Leadership style in project management calls for different approaches, and leaders must be sensitive to
  unique circumstances and personalities.
- The ability to meet motivational requirements depends
  on the capacity to appraise unfulfilled needs and to
  adjust job designs to meet those needs.
- Conflict is effectively dealt with through problem solving or confrontation approaches.
- Participative decision making motivates team members and contributes toward effective decisions.

Optimizing the Human Side of Project Management

How will enhancing the human side of project management
bring about positive project results? How will it help improve
project quality, reduce costs, and ensure that the project
will proceed according to schedule? Here are some of the
ways:

- *Generates synergy.* The arithmetic aberration
"2 + 2 = 5" symbolically illustrates synergy. The term comes
from the field of chemistry, where a mixture of two elements
may produce a result more powerful and significant than
the apparent sum of the original elements. In human interaction, a similar type of reaction often occurs. For instance,
two people cooperating and exchanging ideas will almost
invariably produce more significant results than would the
same two people working separately. Synergy is commonly
illustrated in sports by the "teamwork" concept; a well-
drilled team of unexceptional players who cooperate and
are sensitive to one another's strong and weak points often
overpower a loosely knit group of superstars.

Bear in mind that synergy can also work negatively. In some cases, two plus two might yield a result of *three* rather than five. A task force that fails to "get its act together" might become involved in in-fighting and actually wind up losing ground.

♦ *Builds psychological contracts.* A psychological contract consists of the mutual expectations of the individual and the organization, as articulated by managers; each party brings to the relationship a set of expectations as to what each will give and receive. Sound psychological contracts create an interactive web in which critical activities interface automatically. When open communication exists, mutual expectations are likely to be reasonably compatible. The wise project manager aims at striking sound contracts with team members in hopes of minimizing gaps in expectations.

♦ *Creates a productive setting.* A people-oriented approach to project management is an enjoyable way to perform productive work. Project goals are more likely to be met when a team of motivated professionals works toward achieving objectives that are in harmony with their own professional and personal goals. When give-and-take relationships set the tone for a project and team members believe they are contributing to meaningful project objectives, work becomes more fun. Individuals may actually work harder and longer under a "people" approach than under a systems or other organizational approach.

♦ *Eliminates organizational constraints.* Teams based on a human-side approach to managing projects are less rigid and therefore are more likely to adapt to spontaneous project situations than those based exclusively on a systems approach. If objective psychological contracts have been struck, then team members will have a firm grasp on project objectives and will not allow barriers to stand in the path of progress.

♦ *Improves client relations.* The client's ability to oversee a project, to establish policies, to indicate controls, and to participate in major project decisions is a fundamental factor in a project's success. When the client is perceived as a

group of individuals, each with distinct personal, professional, and project objectives, then client relations tend to
be both harmonious and productive. If relationships are open,
easy, and straightforward, positive results will be forthcom-
ing. If relationships are strained, extended client involvement
will create roadblocks along the project's path.

♦ *Makes project management more effective.* Perhaps the
most important reason for emphasizing the human side of
project management is that it's simply a more effective way
of getting the job done. It paves the way for performing
necessary project tasks by creating an objective problem-
solving atmosphere. The effectiveness of the approach relies
on the principle that all project problems can be solved by
people.

Conclusions

Managing the human factor on projects, where at least half
of the problems reside, can be improved by attaining more
knowledge and skills in behavior-related topics. Although
some people, through natural talent, may already have the
capabilities required in certain areas, any project professional's performance can be boosted to new levels of competence through study and diligence in the areas covered
in the following chapters.

The human side of project management is like a patch-
work quilt—a composite of intangibles that include motivational approaches, conflict management techniques, and
decision-making theories. The human side takes in cross-
cultural subtleties, negotiating strategies, and interfacing
techniques. It includes the behavioral side of planning and
the project manager's special leadership role in managing
people and making decisions. It's aimed at how to achieve
project goals by managing effectively through people, the
project's most valuable resource.

Chapter 2

A Classic View of Project Management

See first that the design is wise and just: that
ascertained, pursue it resolutely; do not for one
repulse forego the purpose that you resolved to
effect.

William Shakespeare

*This chapter gives the classic view of project management.
The human factor approach builds on the foundations of this
classic view. If you want to review the basics—or if you are
new to the field—read on in detail. If, however, you prefer
to concentrate on the human side of managing projects,
thumb through this chapter, then skip to Chapter 3 to begin
your overview of the human side of project management.*

What Project Management Is

How can project management be defined? Is it simply a fast-
tracking management form applied to projects? Or is it
something more complex?

The broad array of fields that use project management techniques set up barriers for defining it. Just as a change of clothes makes a person look different, project management for an experimental education program for underprivileged children looks different from project management for constructing a nuclear power plant. Although organizing a space shot to outer planets may seem to share few management practices with organizing a week-long visit to Mexico for the Pope and his entourage, there are similarities in planning and organizing both undertakings. However, some small projects may be run by the "seat of the pants," using intuitive management techniques, whereas megaprojects call for more formal approaches.

Here are people-oriented definitions that exemplify the concepts used throughout this book:

+ A *project* is a unique venture with a beginning and an end, conducted by people to meet established goals within parameters of cost, schedule, and quality.
+ *Project management* is the combination of people, systems, and techniques required to coordinate the resources needed to complete projects within established goals.

Definitions, however, are generally too condensed to fully capture complex concepts. Just as convenience foods are not easily consumed in concentrated form, curt definitions are often somewhat indigestible, even though they contain all the proper ingredients. To expand on the definition of project management and add substance, volume, and perspective to the concept, a discussion of what project management is and is not follows.

Throughout this book, the term *project management* is used synonymously with *program management*, commonly used by the U.S. Department of Defense and aerospace and electronics industries; *construction management*, preferred in capital construction projects; and *product management*, used in consumer product industries. Although subtle differences in interpretation exist among the terms, for the purposes of our discussion, *project management* is used here as an all-encompassing concept.

Project management is a collection of many things. Just as snapshots taken from different angles help describe a total picture, the following glimpses of project management, when pieced together, constitute an overview.

The Project Management Institute (PMI) takes the position that managing projects consists of effectively dominating eight areas of expertise: scope, time, money (cost), quality, communications, human resources, contracts and supply, and risk management. Although not all authors and professionals agree that these eight categories sum up the essence of project management, the PMI model attempts to organize a body of knowledge necessary to manage projects. Each of the following sections discusses one of these eight areas of project management knowledge.

Managing Scope

Scope refers to boundary definitions of given tasks, activities, contracts, assignments, responsibilities, or missions. It defines where one job ends and another starts. Since most projects are riddled with areas of fuzzy definitions, scope management takes on increased importance. How in fact should scope be managed?—through planning, interfacing, and documentation of items that cross boundaries from one area to another. Much of scope managing can be done through daily coordination and meetings; other scope controls can be achieved through formal procedures, forms, or monitoring systems. Zeroing in on scope helps define exactly what needs to be done by each party, thereby making it easier to reach overall project goals.

Managing Time

The race against the calendar's flipping pages and the ticking of the clock set the tone for project work. This start-to-finish characteristic makes projects stand out from other types of operations; time becomes an important measuring stick for assessing success. For complex projects, sophisticated networking approaches help cope with time; techniques such as PERT/CPM are used in planning and controlling project events.

Centuries before the phrase *project management* was coined, Benjamin Franklin wrote words of counsel that could now be the opening remarks of a project kick-off meeting:

> If time be of all things the most precious, wasting time must be the greatest prodigality, since lost time is never found again; and what we call time enough always proves little enough. Let us then be up and doing, and doing to the purpose; so by diligence shall we do more with less perplexity.[1]

Managing Money

Ultimately, projects can be expressed in monetary terms by summing the costs of equipment, materials, labor, services, real estate, and financing. Even time can be presented in monetary terms. Project management is responsible for controlling overall costs to bring a project in within budgetary constraints. Cash flow management is instrumental in optimizing the use of funds throughout the project's duration. Project teams face both financial and economic balancing acts as they walk the tightrope between budgeted funds and required expenditures. According to Julian Huxley, "We all know how the size of sums of money appears to vary in a remarkable way according as they are being paid in or paid out."[2]

Money is what projects are all about. It's what makes them move ahead, and it's usually the reason for their existence: to generate more money or related benefits for the owner or sponsoring organization.

Managing Quality

Attention to quality is a cornerstone of project management. In industrial projects, standards of quality are spelled out in specifications, which in turn are used as a basis for monitoring project performance. In projects that do not use detailed specifications to lay out explicit quality standards, a minimum functional quality is expected. Pressures from other project elements, such as cost and time, may lead to quality trade-offs, in which quality is compromised in favor of schedule or budget. However, defending project quality always remains a prime project management responsibility.

Managing Communications

Communications on projects take in a range of items— and all need to be adequately managed for the project to be successfully completed. Formal communications require tending to organizational design, strategic planning systems, project planning systems, norms, standards, and procedures. Interpersonal communications also require attention: Do team members have necessary skills for interacting on a daily basis? Then there are communications with the community: Is a public relations effort needed to break down resistance or influence the public? Communication of management information is also a key point: How will the information be organized and communicated between parties—on paper? by electronic mail? in frequent meetings? Communications can make or break a project; managerial attention must be directed at establishing communications channels that will meet the project's needs.

Managing Human Resources

Human resources on projects require managing from three different angles. First, the administrative and bureau-cratic side call for attention to ensure that employee needs are met. These activities include personnel functions, such as recruiting, salary administration, benefits, and vacations. Managing the allocation of manpower is another side of handling human resources on projects. How many people of what qualifications are going to be needed during what period of time on the project? And finally, the motivational and behavioral side of human resources requires managerial attention. What are the needs of the organization? What training and development measures are required? Managing human resources may be the key to meeting all of the other needs on the project, since all actions are ultimately taken by people.

Managing Contracts and Supply

Project management involves dealing with third parties that supply services, material, and equipment. The project's destiny depends on a team's capability in selecting and entering into appropriate contractual terms and in monitoring those third parties. In many instances, managerial and quality-related functions are also passed along to the contracted party. Substantial project management effort must be aimed at picking the right parties to carry out the assignments to be contracted. Then the contractual negotiation must converge on terms that will ensure that the project's needs are met. Finally, a monitoring and expediting effort is required to ensure that the contracting party actually comes through with the promised goods or services within the time frame established and to the specified quality.

Managing Risk

In a stable environment, decisions fall into patterns based on experience, historical data, and practical knowledge. In a no-risk atmosphere of true certainty, routine decisions can be programmed along the following lines: "If a happens, do x; if b happens, do y." Simple rules can be applied and decisions easily made. Decisions made under conditions of risk or uncertainty, however, are not programmable. Under these circumstances, the project setting is characterized by varying environmental conditions, requiring the project team to "problem solve" its way through changing situations. The accuracy of the initial decision depends on the degree of internal and external project uncertainty. The risks that require management on projects include: (1) physical harm or injury; (2) market fluctuations (market demand does not live up to predictions); (3) technological risk (R&D project does not pan out because of inadequate technological premise); and (4) managerial risk (the project pieces simply do not come together, resulting in overruns and poor performance).

Effective Project Management Depends on Systems and People

On all but the smallest projects, systems are needed to steer projects to completion within budget, on time, and within quality parameters. Whether manual, mechanical, or computerized, systems provide procedural and organizational bases for managing daily activities. Systems support project personnel in planning, integrating, and monitoring project fundamentals such as money (using cost control systems or cash flow forecasting), time (using Gantt or PERT/CPM planning and scheduling techniques), and quality (using follow-up, control, and assurance procedures). The systems will be effective provided there is adequate involvement of the people doing the work.

Getting things done through people is project management's major goal. For a project to be successful, people must work together. Team building, conflict management, and communication skills are people-related abilities needed to make project activities work. Everything on a project starts with people. And a project progresses as a result of human interaction.

What Project Management Is Not

As in other human endeavors, misconceptions cloud the air of project management. Two common misconceptions are discussed below.

Project Management Is Not a PERT/CPM Network

PERT/CPM networks and other forms of network diagramming are valuable tools for graphically showing interrelationships among project activities and pinpointing critical tasks. Some managers believe that PERT/CPM systems are so fundamental for achieving project objectives that they constitute the only important management tool. However, equating a PERT/CPM program with project management is analogous to saying that a motor is a car. A project without a good PERT/CPM system is not very effective; yet such a system without other project management tools and practices is just a minor part of a much more significant whole.

Project Management Is Not a Magic Formula

Project management is not a cure-all for solving project problems, and project management techniques will not ensure that a program will move along to a successful conclusion. Each project is unique, so there are no "canned" solutions. Even "packaged" projects, such as thermoelectric power plants, are subject to different environments, geologies, and cultures at each unique site.

Although both a presidential campaign and a back porch add-on to a house are projects sharing certain principles, a detailed formula for managing one will be of little use to the other.

Project's Life Cycle

Common to all projects are the phases characterized by the starting gun, the race itself, and the checkered flag. Projects are marked by a beginning, an end, and some happenings in between, and are said to progress over a life cycle.

A project's life cycle has four distinct phases: (1) conceptual, (2) planning, (3) execution, and (4) termination. Project activity varies sharply over the course of the life cycle: A project starts off slowly, builds up to a peak, and tapers off at its conclusion. (See Figure 2-1.) In an industrial manufacturing project, each phase is typified by the following activities:

1. *The conceptual phase*—includes identifying needs, establishing feasibility, searching for alternatives, preparing proposals, developing basic budgets and schedules, and naming the starting project team.
2. *The planning phase*—involves implementing schedules, conducting studies and analyses, designing systems, building and testing prototypes, analyzing results, and obtaining approval for production.
3. *The execution phase*—encompasses procuring and implementing systems, verifying performance, and modifying systems as required.
4. *The termination phase*—includes training operational personnel, transferring materials, transferring responsibility, releasing resources, and reassigning project team members.

Terminology in life cycle planning can vary considerably. For instance, these same four phases can be called (1) initiation, (2) growth, (3) operations, and (4) shutdown.

Figure 2-1. Activity distribution of a typical project life cycle.

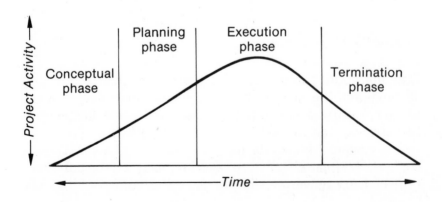

Multidimensional Characteristics

The cube shown in Figure 2–2, conceived with a capital construction project in mind, illustrates the three-way interplay that takes place among the management actions and project tasks.

The first dimension defines what must be done. For capital projects, this includes engineering design, procurement of materials and equipment, and construction or installation of products or facilities. These are measurable work items: Engineering design can be gauged by production of drawings; procurement can be measured by materials purchased; and construction can be assessed by physical work completed.

The cube's second dimension consists of factors that specify project performance levels: cost (budget), schedule (time), and quality (performance). Budgets put a ceiling on funds available to the project. Schedules delimit how and when project tasks will be carried out. Specified quality levels spell out constraints on project performance.

The third dimension features the tools for coordinating the work within the limits of the project. Project management tools include planning, control, and evaluation. Planning involves identifying a work sequence and looking ahead for pitfalls in an attempt to optimize resources. Progress against the plan is monitored by project controls. Finally, deviations between performance and plan are evaluated and acted on by management.

Fast Tracking

Time can be underutilized or optimized. Its value is quantifiable by using Benjamin Franklin's concept of time as money. If a project's completion is delayed, the schedule of the venture's operational phase will be affected, and that phase is presumably designed to generate income or benefits measurable in monetary terms. Conversely, costs incurred during the implementation phase to speed up a project may be more than offset if revenue is generated sooner by meeting

Figure 2-2. The three dimensions of capital project management.

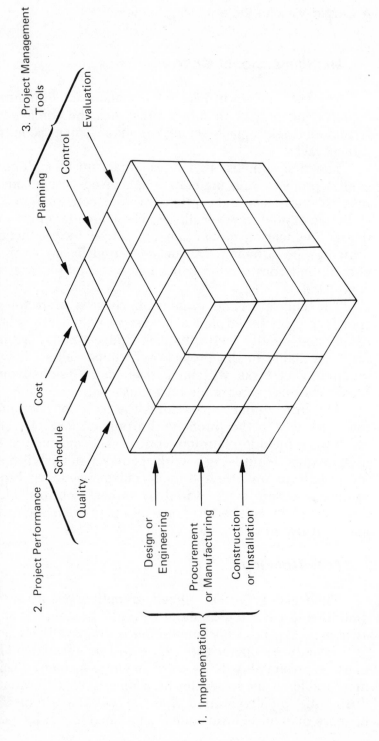

3. Project Management Tools

Planning   Control   Evaluation

2. Project Performance

Quality   Schedule   Cost

Design or Engineering

Procurement or Manufacturing

Construction or Installation

1. Implementation

an earlier operational deadline. Therefore, the monetary value of project time, which can be calculated using standard engineering economics techniques, determines the extent to which the project schedule should be accelerated.

There are two approaches to scheduling: series and phased. If time is not a major constraint, a series schedule, in which each stage is completed before the next one begins, is feasible. However, if the use of time must be optimized, a phased schedule, in which stages overlap, is called for. Phased scheduling is also called fast-track scheduling. In this approach, parts of the design phase are initiated before conceptual planning is finished, materials procurement is kicked off before the design phase is completed, and implementation begins before all materials have been procured or manufactured. Phased programming saves time, and a project is completed earlier using a fast-track program than it would be with a sequential schedule.

The fast-track approach is such an integral part of project management that some people consider the terms synonymous. Whether or not the terms mean precisely the same thing, fast-track scheduling has brought project management of age. Phased programs require expertise in management interfacing, whereas the traditional series schedules do not. Projects laced with interfaces and overlapped activities call for artful application of project management tools and practices. Because cost, schedule, and performance are normally at odds with one another, fast-tracking project management teams must weave their way through both technical and managerial obstacle courses in order to reach project completion.

Work Breakdown Structure

For projects to be planned and controlled, they must be broken down into manageable segments. Tasks must be small enough to be accomplished by those performing them, yet not so small that they become minor details. The *work breakdown structure* (WBS) is a classic hierarchical format for splitting projects into measurable and controllable activities. In the WBS, activities are subdivided into levels people can understand and control.

Once the manageable segments—which ultimately constitute the project—are completed, the overall project is also finished and the WBS has done its job. The WBS is like the powerful rockets that have launched spacecraft: Once their highly significant job is done, they fall by the wayside, retaining no residual value. This occurs because the ultimate operational mission begins when the project is completed, and generally uses separate systems and different operational criteria from the project. The WBS is a managerial means to an end. Its very existence may be irrelevant or unknown to the final user (operator), yet timely project completion depends on its effective use.

The format of the WBS is similar to that of a company organization chart, with the uppermost box of the chart representing the project itself. The WBS is then broken into subsequent phases until the size of activities corresponds to the size of manageable tasks, called work packages. Work packages are specific tasks to be performed within the overall WBS framework. They may be characterized by a document or design, physical equipment or material, or services to be performed.

The number of levels in a WBS depends on the project's size, its complexity, and management's philosophy. Terminology for identifying these successive levels also varies. For example, a four-level WBS might be broken down as follows:

Level 1:   *Overall project*
Level 2:   *Area*
Level 3:   *Group*
Level 4:   *Work Package*

WBS Criteria

The criteria or central theme of a WBS varies from project to project. Here are some of the yardsticks that serve as a basis for breaking a project into work packages:

- *Systems and Subsystems.* These apply to projects that are fundamentally composed of interrelated systems that maintain their individual identities. The breakdown follows a systems format.
- *Technology.* In this case, distinct technologies and disciplines make up the project. Coordination along technological lines is the logical basis for the WBS.
- *Vendor Packages.* When the project is made up of major items to be delivered by suppliers, division by vendor packages may be preferred.
- *Physical Space.* If the project is comprised of various operating facilities that are largely self-contained, breakdown by physical area is a logical option.
- *Organizational Requirements.* Organizational influences may affect the WBS for reasons that seem illogical from a technical standpoint. For instance, trade unions may impose special working rules, or joint venture work may be divided politically or by area of expertise.[3]

A simplified WBS is shown in Figure 2–3. Each item is numbered and named to make it easy for both people and the computer. The WBS shown uses a mixture of criteria. The "Area" level is divided on the basis of physical area, reflecting a distinct spacial segregation. Beginning at the group level, however, the project is broken down by discipline.

The WBS can also be represented in an outline format as shown here:

01.00 Area A
   01.01 Civil Construction A
      01.01.01 Earthwork A
      01.01.02 Foundations and Structures A
      01.01.03 Architectural Finishes A
   01.02 Electromechanical A
      01.02.01 Electrical and Control A
      01.02.02 Piping A

01.02.03 Equipment A
01.02.04 Preoperational Tests A
02.00 Area B
  02.01 Civil Construction B
    02.01.01 Earthwork B
    02.01.02 Foundations and Structures B
    02.01.03 Architectural Finishes B
  02.02 Electromechanical B
    02.02.01 Electrical and Control B
    02.02.02 Piping B
    02.02.03 Equipment B
    02.02.04 Preoperational Tests B

Figure 2-3. Simplified WBS.

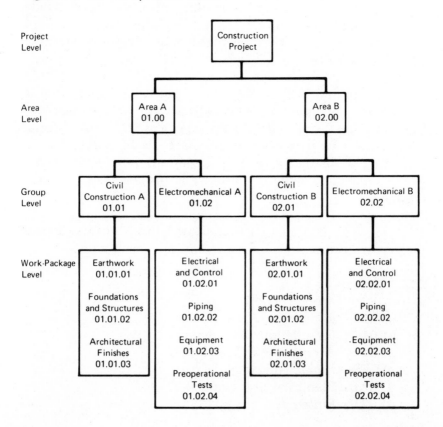

Project Scheduling and Networking Techniques

The WBS is the starting point for project scheduling. Once the work has been packaged in the work breakdown structure, activities must be scheduled so that they can be distributed over the project's life span. There are numerous ways of scheduling projects; techniques can be applied separately or used simultaneously.

Gantt Charts

The Gantt chart, a traditional scheduling technique developed originally for production control, continues to be a highly communicative way for displaying the task and time requirements of a project. The chart shows major activities and a corresponding "bar" or continuous line, which indicates start and completion dates for each activity (see Figure 2–4). Overlapping schedules are clearly shown. In Figure 2–4, the projected schedule is indicated by hollow bars, and the actual schedule by shaded bars.

Gantt charts are used for simplified project planning and scheduling in the following applications.

- The chart makes it possible to get off to a quick start while more sophisticated scheduling techniques are being implemented and debugged.
- Once the project scheduling data have been processed and dates have been fixed according to the project network, the bar chart can be used at field level because of its high readability.
- The chart's simplicity makes it particularly appropriate for summary reporting.

Milestone Charts

Milestones are intermediate achievement dates that stand as guideposts for monitoring a project's progress by singling

Figure 2-4. Simplified Gantt chart for construction project.

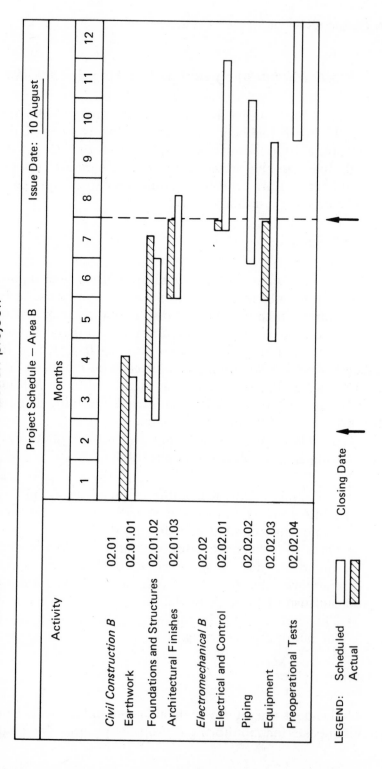

out particularly critical completion deadlines. They are listed on a milestone chart, as shown in Figure 2–5. The milestone chart represents a broad-brush rendering of a project's schedule and control dates.

Project Procedures

Procedures set forth nitty-gritty, step-by-step instructions for guiding a project's activities along their prescribed courses. They constitute the detailed form of project policies and criteria established earlier in the project's life cycle. Procedures reflect a straightforward how-to approach, and include such items as policy statements, checklists, forms, norms, detailed instructions, and charts. Areas typically cov-

Figure 2–5. Simplified milestone chart.

Area B — Project Milestone Status		Date: <u>10 August</u>	
Description of Event	Scheduled Deadline	Actual Date Completed	Delay (Days)
Complete Earthwork B	30 March	15 April	15
Complete Main Foundation Concrete	15 April	30 April	15
Equipment B Received on Site	15 April	15 May	30
Complete Equipment B Foundations	30 May	30 May	0
Piping B Installation, 20% Complete	31 July	—	30
Install Main Transformers	15 August	—	—
Start Area B Preoperational Tests	01 October	—	—
Complete Electromechanical B	01 December	—	—
Complete Tests—Begin Operation	30 December	—	—

ered in project procedure manuals are planning and control, administration, design, project engineering, procurement, manufacturing, and construction.

Project Cost Control

The aim of project cost control is to provide a managerial data base for making timely cost-related decisions during implementation. The cost system can be derived from the work breakdown structure, thus maintaining cost criteria coherent with other project controls. Expenditures are normally compiled in monthly reports that display costs on an item-by-item basis and compare the original budget with the actual cost and with the projected cost to completion. The goal is to spot potential overruns so that management can take necessary and timely countermeasures. A sample reporting format is shown in Figure 2–6.

S-Curve

The S-curve plots the project's expected progress and offers a simple picture of actual versus scheduled advances. It derives its name from the lazy-S shape that the curve takes. On the basis of work hours or monetary amount, a relative weight is assigned to each major activity; the weight represents a percentage of the overall venture. The S-curve, which may be superimposed on the Gantt chart, gives a quick reading of the project's status. An S-curve is shown in Figure 2–7.

Networking

Networking techniques identify interrelationships among activities and optimize project resources. PERT (project evaluation and review technique) and CPM (critical path method) are standard networking approaches. Networking highlights the interdependence among activities and makes it possible to monitor the sequence of the most time-critical activities throughout the project. A complete network resembles a

Figure 2-6. Partial cost control report.

WBS Cost Code	Activity Description Area B— Civil Construction B	Current Month			Cumulative to Date			Cost at Completion		Variance	
		Budgeted Cost	Actual Cost	Variance Over (Under)	Budgeted Cost	Actual Cost	Variance Over (Under)	Budget	Latest Revised Estimate (Projected)	Over (Under)	% of Budget
02.01.01	Earthwork	0	0	0	4,000	6,000	2,000	4,000	6,000	2,000	50%
02.01.01.01	Excavation	0	0	0	2,000	3,500	1,500	2,000	3,500	1,500	75
02.01.01.02	Backfill	0	0	0	2,000	2,500	500	2,000	2,500	500	25
02.01.02	Foundations and Structures	0	500	500	40,000	44,000	4,000	40,000	44,000	4,000	10
02.01.02.01	Formwork	0	0	0	16,000	18,000	2,000	16,000	18,000	2,000	13
02.01.02.02	Rebar	0	0	0	12,000	13,000	1,000	12,000	13,000	1,000	8
02.01.02.03	Embedments	0	0	0	2,000	2,000	0	2,000	2,000	0	0
02.01.02.04	Concrete	0	500	500	10,000	11,000	1,000	10,000	11,000	1,000	10
02.01.03	Architectural Finishes	1,500	1,200	(300)	4,000	3,000	(1,000)	4,000	3,600	(400)	(10)
02.01	Civil Construction B	1,500	1,700	200	48,000	53,000	5,000	48,000	53,600	5,600	12

Figure 2-7. Construction project's schedule and progress, as shown by a Gantt chart with S-curves superimposed.

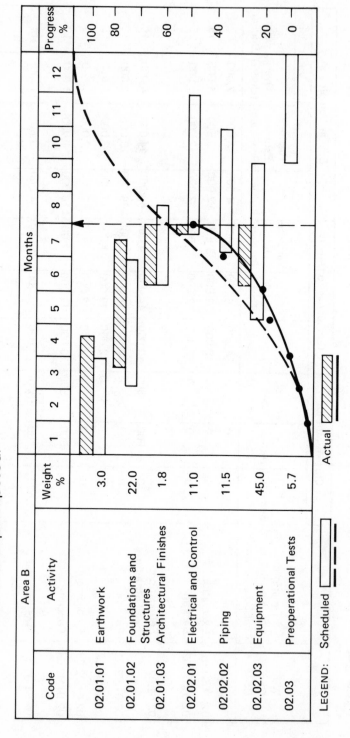

loosely woven fishnet hammock: All paths emerge from one point and converge toward another. In between, the network body, like the hammock, comprises numerous interconnections. A simplified network is shown in Figure 2–8.

What's the Difference Between Project Management and Ongoing Management?

Running projects calls for special managerial approaches to avoid major pitfalls. General managerial principles, while applicable to projects, must be tailored to accommodate each project's unique traits. The special needs of the project team, which are different from those of operations personnel, must also be fulfilled.

Ongoing ventures require long-range planning and marketing, thus creating a setting for long-range survival. Projects are finite, complex, and call for a task-oriented approach. Line and staff relationships in functional organizations are clearly drawn, whereas in projects, task assignments are intermingled in a web of authority and responsibility that is not always clear. In the functional organization, authority is wielded by supervisors over subordinates, whereas on projects, emphasis is given to horizontal and diagonal work flow. In functional structures, objectives are established by the parent unit; in a project atmosphere, on the other hand, goals may be of a multiorganizational nature.

Furthermore, in ongoing organizational structures, the general manager or highest level of authority directs activities. In the typical project, managers operate across functional and organizational lines to accomplish transient goals. The project manager usually carries more responsibility than authority for accomplishing tasks. In functional ongoing organizations, authority and responsibility tend to be more equally balanced. Because managing projects is different from managing ongoing ventures, the special approach called project management is required to meet unique needs.

Figure 2–8. Simplified network for a construction project.

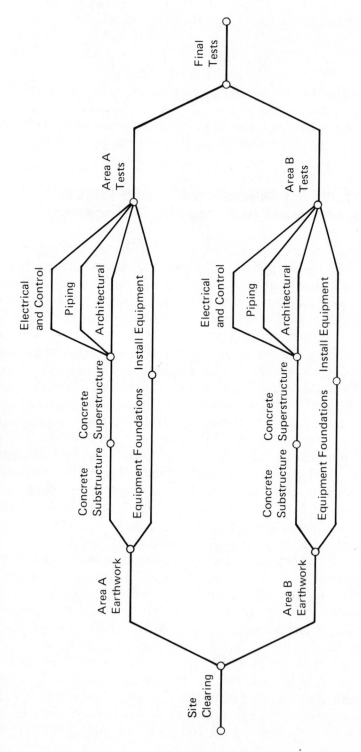

References

1. Cited in Tryon Edwards, *The New Dictionary of Thoughts* (Cincinnati: Standard Book Co., 1977), p. 672.
2. Cited in Laurence J. Peter, *Peter's Quotations* (New York: William Morrow, 1978), p. 345.
3. Charles C. Martin, *Project Management: How to Make It Work* (New York: AMACOM, 1976), p. 121.

Chapter 3

The Project Manager and All

Successful project managers exhibit the traits of Solomon, Job, Mandrake, and the Pied Piper.

Presenting . . . the Project Manager!

Job descriptions for project managers (PMs) spell out attributes, skills, and responsibilities that can only be described as monumental. As a minimum, PMs are required to wind up their projects within established schedule, budget, and quality standards. To achieve their goals, they must marshal often diverging and conflicting resources into harmonious unity.

The PM is supposed to make it all happen by drawing on a well of personal qualities and professional skills. V. E. Cole, former executive vice-president of Kaiser Engineers, has suggested that a construction industry project manager must be all of the following: superb planner, skilled administrator, brass-knuckled fighter, sensitive psychiatrist, gifted engineer, experienced constructor, master of communication, unshakable optimist, super salesperson, and miser.[1] A comparable list of characteristics also applies to PMs of high technology manufacturing projects and of "soft" ventures such as social or educational programs. No matter what the project's nature, the PM must have a full bag of tricks packed with experience in technology, management, and the behavioral arts and sciences.

Such stiff job qualifications raise certain fundamental questions: Can such a job really be handled by a mere human being? Is the burden too big to shoulder? Is it delusory to imagine a project manager sufficiently endowed with talents to efficiently discharge such a wide array of responsibilities? Former Secretary of Commerce Alfred Kann raised just such a question in his keynote speech at the Eleventh Project Management Institute Symposium. With tongue in cheek, he wondered aloud if the project manager's job was not analogous to "certain high-level government positions" where a peculiar paradox presented itself. According to Kahn, some positions are so challenging that "you can't give the job to anyone stupid enough to take it."[2] Kahn's paradox highlights the increasingly difficult task of matching up complex, demanding projects with the mere mortals who are supposed to manage them.

Titles and Names

In real life applications, what is the person in charge of the project actually called? He or she is called by many names—not all of which are complimentary in explosive project environments. Following are some formal titles often assigned:

Product manager
Brand manager
Program coordinator
Project leader
Business manager
Planning director
Systems designer
Task force chairperson
Project administrator

Project coordinator
Task manager
Project engineer
Project manager
Program manager
Executive program manager
Director of programs
Vice-president program development
Contract manager
Construction manager
Implementation manager

The wide spectrum of titles suggests that while project management functions share common responsibilities, the stereotyped character called the project manager in the literature may not exist at all. Just as there is no such thing as a "typical manager" or an "average worker," the project manager as cited in professional publications is perhaps only a model or a prototype against which individuals in project management positions can compare themselves.

There is, however, one common thread that unites all project managers' jobs: the PM's fundamental responsibility for fostering project integration.

To direct a quality endeavor to a timely and economical conclusion, the project manager must act as a resource integrator; project resources such as people, facilities, materials, equipment, and information must be coordinated and integrated so that project goals are met and daily activities maintain the project's momentum. This holds true for software projects, social programs, product development, and major capital undertakings, whether the projects are small, medium-size, or large-scale.

The Project Manager's Woes

PESSIMIST: Project managers are plagued with troubles.
OPTIMIST: Project managers are blessed with opportunities to solve problems.

Whether the prevailing view of the PM's job be woeful or rose-colored, there is little doubt that the position presents almost overwhelming challenges. Most major projects are strongly influenced by factors such as external policies, preferences and opinions of the clients, joint venture partners, general contractors, financing institutions, government agencies, and outside experts. Within the PM's own organization, internal political pressures and power struggles are also part of the project's challenge. Other project management troubles may be brought on by the numerous ambiguous situations that appear during the project's life cycle.

Responsibility vs. Authority

Project managers charged with attaining ambitious goals often lack sufficient formal authority to meet them. In most cases, the PM is unable to *order* all project-related people to promptly swing into cadence and expeditiously perform the activities required to keep the project on track. For instance, the PM may have little or no authority over (1) functional managers, (2) client personnel, and (3) local officials; yet, without the cooperation of these parties, it's unlikely that the project's goals will be met. In spite of an inevitable authority gap, the project manager is expected to move mountains to meet objectives. By nature, the job already represents an immense challenge and the responsibility/authority mismatch makes the task even tougher.

The mismatch between the responsibilities shouldered and the formal authority available might be intentional because of company culture or prior project successes. Or it might be the inadvertent result of a lack of awareness or experience. In companies that have flexible horizontal communication and a solid project-completion record, formal charters establishing authority may be unnecessary or even undesirable. In contexts in which a project-oriented culture is not predominant, clearly defined authority for the PM may be the key to success. The manager's own perception of the relationship between responsibility and authority also influences the way projects are run. For instance, the PM who tends to rely heavily on formal authority will be un-comfortable working on projects in which responsibility far exceeds authority. If, however, the mismatch is accepted as part of the game, the PM stands a good chance of finding ways to enhance authority and thus exert an increased influence over the project's destiny.

The Interactive Challenge

The project manager's job is complicated by the sheer number of key people and groups that demand attention. For instance, functional departments require routine inter-vention to maintain technical continuity and keep personnel attuned to overriding project objectives. Staff groups reach out for attention and orientation. The PM's supervisors must be kept up-to-date on the project's overall status. The project manager's role involves coordinating internal actions with the outside environment, which often means dealing with government officials and public interest groups. The client, whether an outside entity or an in-house group, consumes the PM's time in activities such as reporting on the project's status, making decisions about policies, and routine stroking. The project team interacts constantly with the PM as well, carrying out the procedures required to achieve the project's goals. Subcontractors, outside consultants, and other third parties are also part of the PM's parade of relationships.

Each party perceives the project in its own distinct way and attempts to influence the course of events by bringing pressure to bear on the project manager. This pressure is felt in forms ranging from gentle nudges to brass-knuckled power plays. The PM's ability to deal with each situation as it occurs, and to avoid major problems through planning and interfacing with key parties, increases the probability of achieving the project's goals.

The Project Sponsor

The project sponsor is usually the person or group to whom the project manager reports within the parent organization. In some cases, the sponsor may maintain a matrix relationship with the PM. The project sponsor provides support, nurtures high-level contacts, and monitors the project's overall performance. Ultimate responsibility for project success resides with the project sponsor, whose job also includes assigning the PM to the job in the first place—and removing him or her if necessary. It is the project sponsor's function to fix the PM's authority/responsibility charter. That charter may be (1) formally established per standing procedures, (2) negotiated specifically for the project at hand, or (3) left to a loose, informal understanding. The project sponsor's perception of what the role is influences the PM's behavior. For instance, if the sponsor sees the manager's position as one of great authority, then the PM can walk tall and wield power with appropriate dispatch. On the other hand, if the charter is unclear or inadequately communicated, authority may be perceived in a markedly humbler light.

The Client

Whether a project is being undertaken for a third-party client, such as a power company, manufacturing firm, or government agency, or work is being performed in-house for another group residing under a common corporate roof, the PM must work to establish a special relationship with the client. After all, the client is the ultimate boss. It's the client who, in the final analysis, pays the bills and therefore must be satisfied.

Yet the PM's role, though it's supposed to be well defined in contractual terms, may be perceived in varying ways by clients. If client personnel are laid back in nature, they may expect the PM to take initiative and act with rapid, bold strokes. An aggressive client who takes a hands-on approach may cause the PM to shift toward a more participative stance, requiring extensive prior discussion of proposed decisions with interested client personnel. The project's success is strongly dependent on the PM's ability to conciliate project management philosophies with the client.

The Project Team

The PM's performance is affected by the project team's actions. The project team works directly with the PM in performing planning, coordination, interfacing, and control functions. A high-energy group of objective professionals can boost the PM to new heights of effectiveness. A below-caliber group, however, will drain the PM's energies until corrective action, in the form of training, motivation, or substitution, can be taken.

In an appeal asking project managers to delegate work to the project team, H. Murray Hohns, former president of the Project Management Institute, once stated dramatically about effective PMs, "Project managers do no work. None!"[3] If this is true, then the PM's interactive role with the project team, and the image projected to that team, are particularly critical, because the actual project work itself is largely delegated and must be carried forth by project team members.

Functional Groups

Functional groups represent, in essence, pools of expertise able to handle specific work tasks and provide basic project support. A systems department with the knowledge and ability necessary to set up project programming and controls is an example of a functional group. The operations division and the civil engineering department are other examples. Functional groups are ongoing—they normally last as long as the company does—and this characteristic sets functional groups apart from project teams, which are transient in nature. Functional personnel tend to be long-term employees generally concerned with professional growth within the functional group over an extended period of time. The project manager, a transient figure, must have the sensitivity and ability to inspire functional personnel to make the effort needed to bring the project to a successful conclusion.

Third Parties

Third parties in project development include government organs, consultants, contractors, suppliers, and service-company vendors. *Government third parties* may include licensing and approval bodies. The PM has no direct control over these groups but must help create effective relationships with them so that the project can move along on course. *Contracted third parties*, on the other hand, generally perform the actual physical work required to finish a project. On an industrial construction job, for example, they manufacture the equipment, pour the concrete, and make the physical connections. On a systems project, they design and install the system, perform the tests, and de-bug the initial operation.

In other words, the real physical work on projects is usually done by others, not by the PM or project management team members. As a matter of fact, the project management team generally performs no work which can be tangibly perceived upon project completion. All end-result tasks that can be seen or touched are likely to have been performed by someone else. Direct project action, therefore, is concentrated within the third parties' work scope. The PM and project management team provide intangibles, such as managing, planning, interfacing, coordinating, following up, and controlling, so that others can carry out their tangible tasks within the grand design of the project.

The Project Manager's Parallel Loyalties

Most project managers are required to wear several different hats. Talented PMs may even have a flair for wearing their hats simultaneously and with style. Each hat corresponds to a specific loyalty, and the PM, by definition, must be strongly pledged to each of these allegiances. The PM's principal loyalties are:

- ◆ *Loyalty to profession.* If, for instance, the PM is heading up a major engineering endeavor, then prime allegiance is owed to the engineering profession and its ethics in order to ensure a safe and technically sound final product.

+ *Loyalty to client.* Because the client controls the purse strings and is usually the owner of the project, the PM must be loyal to the client's best interests.

+ *Loyalty to parent organization.* The PM's paycheck comes from the parent organization and his or her career moves forward within that organization. As the PM's employer, the parent organization deserves fidelity.

Maintaining loyalty to all parties is a delicate balancing act requiring conviction, naturalness, and finesse.

The PM and Macro-Issues

The challenges facing the project manager are perhaps even more profound than they initially seem. Day-to-day trials, ambiguities, and problems are plentiful, yet these represent individual trees in a large forest. The nature of project management philosophies and project tools change with time as the world moves through new economic, social, and technological cycles. Project managers must be increasingly prepared to take on the challenges as transitions occur. They must be geared for changes that will occur, both in fast-tracking projects and in the world.

During the manager's professional lifetime, project management philosophies, practices, and techniques are bound to undergo striking mutations. For example, graphic presentations have evolved from simple bar charting into sophisticated network-based systems. Site-selection decisions used to be straightforward; now they may involve compiling reams of reports to meet state and national legal requirements. The PM must stay attuned to trends in order to keep skills and knowledge sharpened and to ensure both professional success and personal survival.

The PM's Job

Just how is the PM supposed to make it through this professional and environmental obstacle course? What techniques will ensure the project's success? What really is the project manager's job? Not much of substance has been added to the list of basic management functions presented in 1916 by the French industrialist Henri Fayol: planning, organizing, coordinating, and controlling.[4] If those functions are carried out adequately, whatever is being managed will probably reach satisfactory performance levels; Fayol's principles are fundamentally universal and apply to all types of management, whether ongoing or transitory.

But do managers indeed perform the basic managerial functions? The nature of the manager's job, as outlined in the classic literature, is basically reflective in nature, whereas studies show that managers are generally action-oriented and tend to shy away from reflective work. The plan-organize-coordinate-control functions are not what managers actually do, but simply the objectives managers have when they work. Managers actually develop three fundamental roles. First is the *interpersonal role*, which includes the figurehead, leadership, and liaison functions. Second, the manager performs an *informational role*, which involves disseminating information and acting as a spokesperson. The third role is that of the *decision maker*, in which the manager acts as entrepreneur, resource allocator, and negotiator.[5] These roles, as outlined, are also broad in scope and generally apply to any management situation.

There are two principles, however, unique to project management. First, project management is set apart from traditional management by the "mortality" of project work, the fact that projects have finite life cycles. Second, there are widely varying views as to how project management should actually be performed. From the listing of project managers' titles given earlier in this chapter, it is clear that the job cannot be stereotyped. In trying to "zero in" on the nature of the project manager's job, each specific project must be carefully scrutinized. Does the job call for a task force project manager? What are the client's expectations? How has this type of project been handled before? What are the cultural or structural limitations?

Here are some of the project manager's roles that fit under the umbrella of project management. All of them can effectively meet project needs when the role is properly cast and played.

Project Activator

The project activator struggles against tough odds. Little authority is available and the project's organizational structure is often unclear. The activator is expected to work almost magically within a functional hierarchy where horizontal mobility is severely limited. The project activator, who generally works from a staff position, is sometimes seen as a glorified expeditor or "follow-upper." However, depending on the activator's technical expertise and behavioral skills, the role can be expanded to increase effectiveness. Here are some tips for managing from the project activator's position:

- *Know your charter.* Reach a formal or informal understanding with your superior regarding your functions; define what you are expected to accomplish and what resources you have to do the job.
- *Tread lightly.* Since you are dealing with others who wield superior power, move smoothly and cautiously.
- *Ask for counsel.* To overcome resistance, take complex issues to the most influential parties involved, asking for ideas and guidance; then incorporate their input as much as possible in your solution.
- *Build bridges.* Be especially helpful, do favors, build a stockpile of goodwill.
- *Work together.* Create control systems and other coordinating tools jointly with involved parties; ask for opinions and approvals.

♦ *Know your project.* Boost your influence by thoroughly understanding the project. Don't try to compete, however; use your knowledge to help guide the work.
♦ *Encroach.* All projects have a need for an effective project manager. And this requires a reasonable level of influence. Once basic groundwork and relationships are established, strive toward increasing your power base through the authority of competence and the authority of relationships.

Project Coordinator

The project coordinator has a stronger authority charter than the project activator. Coordinators are often assigned to centralize contacts with a client or other outside parties. The coordinator is recognized as a significant project player, in spite of obscure lines of authority. The coordinator's posture may vary, however, from the weak stance of a "communications coordinator" involving re-routing and following up on project correspondence, to a *de facto* project manager position in which influence has been raised to a higher level.

Although the project coordinator's position is more forceful than the activator's, the tips listed previously also apply. As in the case of the activator, the project coordinator is "hierarchically inferior" to the functional managers participating on the project. The fundamental difference is that the coordinator starts with a stronger authority charter. Whether this initial power base is enhanced or eroded, however, depends on each individual coordinator's ability.

Matrix Project Manager

Project managers operating in matrix settings also face ambiguous situations and lack full authority to carry out management responsibilities. As opposed to the activator and coordinator, however, the classic matrix project manager has *equal* status with corresponding functional managers. The role, therefore, calls for strong peer-level negotiating abilities.

Matrix managers must know where to find help and must have a knack for convincing functional and support groups to provide needed resources on a timely basis.

The matrix organization is thus characterized by a "two-boss" situation. One of the bosses is the project manager, who determines what is to be done and when to do it. The other boss is the functional manager, who orients people on how things are to be done and identifies the resources required. The project manager concentrates on defining work activities and schedules, while the functional manager is concerned with quality assurance and technical competence. Here are some tips for project managers who work within a matrix structure:

1. *Understand the power structure.* Analyze and work on relationships with influential members of upper management; achieve a mutual understanding about the nature of your job.
2. *Build alliances with functional managers.* Think of functional managers as fellow members of a team. Smooth interplay and dynamic rapport are needed for the team (and team members) to win the game.
3. *Be flexible.* "There's more than one way to skin a cat" goes the saying. If functional groups suggest an acceptable way to meet a need and are enthusiastic about it, let them move ahead, even if your own approach is different. That way, you avoid hassles and build goodwill.
4. *Be prepared to shift.* The matrix balance of power tends to shift as the project moves through its life cycle. Functional managers dominate activities in the beginning, before the project manager becomes entrenched. During the middle phases, which require concentrated dynamic interfacing, the PM tends to emerge as the primary project leader. Then, as the phase-out stage draws near, functional managers regain their previously predominant positions.
5. *Push for progress.* The project manager's job is to make things happen. If the functional watchdogs are

in place, technical quality is assured. The project manager's main thrust then must be to push through bureaucratic barriers and see that activities are pursued on a timely and cost-effective basis.

Task Force Project Manager

For the task force project manager, lack of power or authority is not a major issue; other project constraints tend to take on larger proportions. For instance, mobilizing and demobilizing personnel becomes a major challenge; maintaining appropriate technical expertise may prove difficult in a task force operation; the cost of the task force may be questioned because of the inherent difficulty of fully optimizing the assigned human resources; the task force may assume responsibilities that, in other project management forms, would be shared with others. Here are some suggestions for the task force project manager:

1. *Secure the commitment of upper management.* Through negotiation, establish your project's charter with higher management and obtain commitment for resources and support.
2. *Watch quality.* Build quality assurance into your organization design. Run periodic quality audits.
3. *Think people.* Since you're on your own, the quality of project personnel will make or break the project. Keep tabs on top people and build a recruiting network to ensure that key spots are well filled.
4. *Control the costs of project management services.* Watch for burgeoning costs resulting from an overgrown organization. Start phasing down on a timely basis.

In each type of leadership role—as activator, coordinator, matrix PM, and task force PM—the leader faces different challenges. Individual project managers, therefore, may be more successful in one role than in another. For instance, an effective project activator might be incapable of running a strong task force, just as a good task force PM might fit poorly into the activator slot.

No standard description is adequate to outline the subtle variations encompassed by the project manager's job. There *is*, however, a set of classic goals for all project management positions. The PM is always responsible for bringing the project to completion to the satisfaction of the sponsoring parties and within the parameters of time (schedule), cost (budget), and quality (performance). This part of the job is a constant for all PMs. What varies is the authority the project manager has to carry out that feat, which may range from almost nil for the activator to a lot but not enough for the task force manager. The job remains largely the same, but the techniques for attaining the goals must be custom tailored to fit the specific project.

Theoretically, goals can be met under any of these project leadership modes simply by applying Fayol's general principles of planning, organizing, coordinating, and controlling. Yet, in project management, it has been shown that a strong *managerial behavior* slant is needed to actually carry out those basic tasks and adapt them to special project situations. The skills and abilities needed to perform the project management job are examined by Thamhain and Wilemon, who group them into six major categories:

1. Leadership:
   - Clear direction and leadership
   - Participating in technical problem solving and decision making
   - Clearly delineating goals and objectives
   - Unifying team toward project goals
   - Delegating
   - Sound decision making
2. Technical expertise:
   - Understanding the technologies involved in the design, development, production, and fielding of the project
   - Understanding of applications, markets, and customer requirements

- Managing technology
- Assessing risks and trade-offs
- Predicting technological trends
- Assisting in problem solving
- Communicating effectively with technical team

3. Human skills:
   - Building multidisciplinary teams
   - Involving and stimulating personnel
   - Managing conflict
   - Communicating both orally and in writing with all levels of personnel
   - Fostering a work environment conducive to teamwork
   - Involving senior management

4. Administrative skills:
   - Project planning
   - Resource negotiations
   - Securing commitments
   - Assuming measurable milestones
   - Establishing operating procedures
   - Establishing and maintaining reporting and review systems
   - Establishing and managing project controls
   - Effective use of program management tools and techniques
   - Effective manpower planning

5. Organizational skills:
   - Understanding how the organization works and how to work with the organization effectively
   - Building multifunctional work teams
   - Working effectively with senior management
   - Understanding organizational interfaces
   - Setting up an effective project organization

6. Entrepreneurial skills:
   - General management perspective
   - Managing a project as a business
   - Meeting profit objectives
   - Developing new and follow-on business[6]

In the detailed breakdown of characteristics and abilities given, it is significant to note that behavioral interaction is a major theme running throughout all the skill categories— even the category called technical expertise.

Staying Proactive

The PM's success depends largely on the ability to remain proactive. Staying ahead of the herd makes the leadership task much simpler. David Starr Jordan, first president of Stanford University, put it this way in his oft-quoted saying: "The world steps aside, makes a path for the man who knows where he's going."[7] Cervantes said it another way: "Each is the maker of his own good fortune."[8] A proactive stance means leading the project to its goals as opposed to pushing and shoving tasks to completion. Being proactive means coming up with new ideas and different approaches. It calls for being creative, receptive, and ever at the forefront, looking ahead to clear the path for important project activities. It signifies generating joint concern, active participation, and team spirit. A proactive posture means that action verbs must be part of the PM's style, with particular attention given to words called the "ates": delegate, estimate, participate, investigate, isolate, dedicate, delineate, compensate, accelerate, instigate, evaluate, obligate, advocate, agitate, correlate, attenuate, eliminate, generate, nominate, discriminate, communicate, and differentiate. Proacting means thinking in action-related terms and transforming those thoughts into end results.

The Three-Pronged Thrust for Managing Successful Projects

Successful managers generally use a three-pronged attack for managing projects, concentrating on (1) project objectives, (2) client relations, and (3) parent-company objectives. Failure to make points in any of these areas can lead to the downfall of even the most talented PM. While other project-success variables might be unearthed by using a different breakdown, or other semantics, project success depends fundamentally on simultaneously managing these related, yet distinct, areas. This can be done by adhering to the following principles:

1. Hold true to the basics. Be diligent in pursuing the overall project goals of schedule, cost, and quality/performance.
2. Remember the retailer's motto: "The customer is always right." See that the customer gets a good product and is pleased with the service.
3. Carefully manage the project management services agreement—whether performed for an outside client or an in-house customer—in the best commercial interests of your parent organization. Be aware of opportunities for increasing profits or achieving other benefits.

References

1. V. E. Cole, presentation to a group of Project Management Institute members visiting Raymond Kaiser Engineers, Inc., Oakland, Calif., October 10, 1982.
2. Alfred Kahn, keynote address to the Project Management Institute Symposium, Atlanta, Ga., October 17, 1979.
3. H. Murray Hohns, "What Does Your Viewpoint of Project Manager Include?" Plenary Session of Project Management Institute Symposium, Toronto, October 4, 1982.
4. Henri Fayol, *Administração Industrial e Geral* (São Paulo, Brazil: Editora Atlas S.A., 1967), p. 12.
5. Henry Mintzberg, "The Manager's Job: Folklore and Fact," *Harvard Business Review* (July–August 1975), pp. 54–56.

6. Hans J. Thamhain and David L. Wilemon, "Developing Project/Program Managers," *Project Management Institute Proceedings* (October 1982), pp II-B.3–4. Adapted by permission.
7. As quoted by Bernard Haldane in *Career Satisfaction and Success* (New York: AMACOM, 1974), p. 81.
8. *Ibid.*, p. 135.

Chapter 4

Project Blending: Building the Project Team

I have a comment for the project managers.
I've been on eleven projects now, and never
have been to an orientation program of what
the project is about or what it is supposed to
accomplish.

**Anonymous Observation at Fourteenth Project
Management Institute Seminar/Symposium**

Project Cooking

Anyone who has ever watched a good cook in action knows
that a well-timed stir can make the difference between a
savory sauce and a swilly broth. Through experience, training, or instinct, the cook knows when to add a special dash
to bring about that certain taste.

Projects, like foods, also respond to a special touch. When
project ingredients are artfully blended, the result is a successful venture that meets the yardstick of a quality project
completed within budget and on time. On the other hand,

without a synergistic stir, project pieces may be left in a muddle where anything can happen. This, in turn, may lead to a sharp decline in project productivity.

A well-blended project "jells" when a sense of teamwork exists; that in turn influences the degree of perceived project success or failure. Different projects in the U.S. space program showed sharply different degrees of cooperative effort among project members. Erasmus H. Kloman observed: "Lunar Orbiter benefited from a strong sense of teamwork within both the customer and contractor organizations and in their relations with each other. Surveyor was handicapped by the lack of an equivalent sense of teamwork, particularly in the early years of the program."[1]

All the right ingredients don't necessarily make a great cake. In the project world, this maxim rings true. For instance, a carefully selected group of highly competent specialists might not make the best team. Likewise, great scheduling and control systems might even be prejudicial if the project group is accustomed to other approaches and doesn't want to change. And standards and procedures may simply gather dust if the project ambience isn't right.

Optimizing project resources is easily done on paper, but only a well-primed team working together to achieve common goals can make it happen. *Project blending* is the mixing and mingling of project ingredients so they are united intimately. Because displacement of project resources is governed by people (key project personnel), the secret of successful project blending is to first establish a good mix of project people. These people take care of mixing the remaining ingredients to meet project goals. The trick is to come up with the right blend of key people to direct and nurture the project to successful completion.

This basic issue sparks other pertinent questions, such as: How can an atmosphere be created that guarantees that the right project moves will be made at the right time? How can the group be motivated so that reaching project goals will take priority over blindly following rigid rules and lines of responsibility? How can forays be made into the blurry territory of project interface that allow for quick retreats to home territory without incurring inordinate casualties? How can a project tone be established that sends a constant and subliminal message of objectivity?

If the answers to these questions are not at least partially available, the project may find itself frequently facing failure, which may appear on a regular or random basis throughout the project's life span. Projects that lack proper blending are bound to run into trouble. Here are sample situations in which the right project mix does not exist:

♦ A multimillion-dollar construction project starts out on an amiable note. Competent people fill the key spots. During the first few months the project moves slowly because the clients drag their feet. Soon project milestones are moved aside as the schedule becomes impossible to meet and in-fighting breaks out at all levels in the project. The project heads into a tailspin and the "witchhunt" to find the guilty parties begins.

♦ Several different cultures are mixed on one project. Blacks, Hispanics, and WASPs of various nationalities are targeted to benefit from an urban renewal project. A "community board" is set up to oversee the project, which will be managed by city authorities. From the start, the community board splits into cultural sub-groups that struggle diligently, with little success, toward making consensus decisions. The board stalemates and fades into the background as city authorities decide to proceed as they see best. Community support flags even more, and before it is off the ground the program is thwarted by community indifference and accusations of mismanagement.

♦ Project "M" has been on the drawing board for years. A major industrial giant has decided to "go matrix," swinging its managerial posture from the traditional pyramidal hierarchy to a more flexible "horizontal" approach. Extensive studies showed the rewards the company would reap by making the move. The board of directors called in upper management to formalize the decision and jointly sent out an "administrative norm" to all departments, regional offices, and subsidiaries. Although the new organization was spelled out in great detail (including revised responsibilities and duties for key personnel), six months after the announcement, company morale was at an all-time low and productivity was plummeting.

In the three cases cited, the effects of a weak project mix border on the catastrophic. One case was characterized by foot-dragging, another by mixed-culture noncommunication, and the third by an internal organizational shuffle. Absent in these examples was a conscious effort early in the project to integrate all parties.

High Stakes

In the aftermath of a poorly blended project, project management's high stakes are starkly spotlighted. Heads roll in the search to find the guilty. The project manager and staff members are particularly likely candidates, but anyone may be blamed for a project's troubles. For instance, contracts may be combed by a client bent on imposing sanctions or penalties. Even if this doesn't come to pass, it's no fun being defensive when energies are needed to work toward meeting project goals.

Scorched reputations are often the upshot of the projects gone astray. All those associated with failing ventures can be tainted—even when they're not directly involved in running the projects. The client (or upper management for in-house projects) is ultimately responsible for a project's success. Basic project decisions are either made or ratified by the client or upper-management personnel, who therefore become jointly embroiled in the prevailing project mire. Outside consultants, architects and engineers, and contractors are also hit by the unmerciful backlash caused by hung-up projects. No one comes out unscathed; all key groups suffer and some may even be irreparably burned.

In spite of the problems that arise in unblended projects, program proposals aimed at toning down the problems are often met with indifference. And such programs must be carried out early in the project in order to achieve optimum results. However, if problems haven't yet surfaced, proposals favoring the organization of a "project integration program," for example, may fall on apathetic ears. To some hardened project professionals, integration programs featuring participative discussions or management seminars may smack of "frilly academics." Even when the climate is more favorable and opposition is not as clear cut, project team-building programs are often "sandbagged" into oblivion by the pressure of other priorities. Poorly blended projects are apt to get off to slow starts. The unintegrated project starts poorly and tends to drag its failures through the entire project.

Team-building programs are not the solution to starting projects effectively. No one can bake a cake (or mount a project) without the right ingredients. An inspiring round of seminars, therefore, is not a cure for faulty conceptual planning or understaffing; a round table discussion will not assure that the planning and scheduling system will be adequately designed. To come up with the right blend, basic project elements must be present. Team-building efforts are designed to work catalytically with those elements—to make them interact and spawn the desired results.

On the other hand, with the right project manager, the extra synergistic push to make things happen may not be needed at all—the manager can simply add the timely dashes that yield the best blend. While this is possibly a valid concept, the "right project manager" is becoming a rare creature. With spiraling technological and cultural complexities and multibillion-dollar ventures involving several countries and multiple currencies, a single human's capacity for managing projects is indeed taxed. Even on smaller projects, a project manager's individual talents are often outmatched by technological or behavioral intricacies.

The logical approach, therefore, is to try to blend the talents of key project personnel so that they react to project challenges the way a well-trained basketball team does. Each person's strong points are maximized, each knows how to cover for the others, and each has a feel for what teammates will do in a given situation. Special team magic occurs when players work together to master the fundamentals.

How to Blend Project Elements

What is the best way to blend the talents of key project personnel? How can it be done most effectively to meet project needs? Who should be involved? Should the programs be extended to various project levels and include all major participating parties? When should blending be done? Who should do it?

"It all depends" is the classic answer to these questions. It depends on the project, the people, the place, and the time. There aren't any pat answers in project management; each situation is a special case and must be assessed on its own merits. A custom-fitted suit is tailored based on certain principles and rules of thumb, yet it's cut to the measurements of the person being fitted. The right blend of project talents depends on the decision maker's ability to custom-tailor a project to meet specific needs.

The project manager or other key party striving for the right mix has a wide array of techniques to choose from. They range from simple one-on-one coaching sessions to sophisticated multiphased development programs. In between are short courses, project games, lectures, round table discussions, and seminars, which can be used separately or in combinations. The panoply of blending techniques is as broad as the imagination allows and includes any and all approaches that promote development of project interaction skills. The following major categories are commonly used techniques: setting examples, coaching, conducting training sessions, and using formal team-building programs.

Setting Examples

All managers communicate their management philosophies to some extent by setting both overt and subliminal examples. The project manager who trusts subordinates and delegates authority to key project members can expect others to emulate that style. Likewise, an open give-and-take approach by the manager will foster similar behavior in the project team and in others associated with the project. Through the project manager's own actions, the key members' best behavior can be elicited.

This "multiplier effect" can result in increasing productivity. The extent to which a manager will be emulated, however, is limited by the individual's personal store of managerial traits. Some personal traits are inherent (charisma and strong leadership characteristics, for example), whereas other abilities can be developed over time (motivating, negotiating, and conflict managing). The ability to set a good example, therefore, is a great aid to blending project elements *if* the manager possesses the qualities required.

Coaching

"No man can reveal to you ought but that which already lies half asleep in the dawning of your knowledge," said Kahlil Gibran.[2] A concentrated and personalized method for drawing out the knowledge that resides drowsily within is called the "coaching approach." A coaching session can be as simple as a chat with a subordinate who made a mistake about why it happened and what can be done to keep it from recurring. Or it can be a formal interview by the manager, who goes into the session with a tailor-made approach. Yet another type of coaching uses classic management tools such as position descriptions and performance standards. The project's goals can be discussed with subordinates while negotiating the final wording of these instruments.

Coaching is usually done by the project manager. But anyone can slip on the coach's cap to try to arrange human behavioral patterns in harmony with the pace of the project machine. Project "advisory council" members, key client representatives, project consultants, and team members may all be required to test their coaching skills from time to time. Coaching can be done with subordinates, with peers, and even with superiors.

The Chat

Most key management personnel coach others without even realizing it. They do it intuitively. They may be simply discussing a problem or searching for a solution, but the "chat" can convey precious gems of project wisdom if it's carried out within the proper context and on the right cue. Chats, by nature, are often impromptu, unrehearsed encounters. The results of such endeavors are often frankly positive, as a manager can take advantage of the moment to emphasize a given point. On the other hand, the chat sometimes falls short of its mark because the topic under discussion hasn't been thoroughly thought out.

Since the coaching chat is aimed at correcting or adjusting behavior patterns, a mental walk-through can help crystallize the discussion so it accomplishes its purpose. Chats normally dispense with formal preparation, yet some questions should be considered beforehand:

- Is the timing right? Is today the right day to broach the subject?
- How deep should you go into the subject? Should you deal with it superficially, in-depth, mid-way?
- What kind of approach should you use? Should you lecture, listen, or encourage give and take?
- What really motivates the person? What are the person's most important goals? What stimulates the person's interest?
- What are the benefits to the person if behavior is changed? Greater earnings, a "pat on the back," increased status?
- What kind of person are you chatting with? Uptight, aggressive, shy?

In-Depth Coaching

Taking a deeper dive into project coaching means working out strategy on paper. Mentally "winging it" won't do the trick. Real planning is needed for a coaching session to be productive. In-depth coaching requires probing into the following subjects: What makes the other individual tick? What kind of benefit does the person expect for changing behavior? What approaches will be most effective in reaching the person? What are the best motivators when dealing with the person?

Consider the following questions when preparing an in-depth coaching session:

+ What is your relationship with the other person involved in the interaction? Are you that person's superior, peer, subordinate?
+ What characteristics predominate in the individual? Aggressiveness, cautiousness, sociability, objectivity?
+ What might cause the individual to change behavior? Recognition, high- or low-risk situations, appeasing situations, challenge, chance for improvement?
+ What is the best approach to use in conducting the session—structured or loose agenda?
+ What is the reason or objective for the meeting?
+ What benefit can you offer the other person? That the person won't be fired, will get a new challenge, will reduce personal risk, will gain recognition?
+ What is the best approach to tell whether the message was received and accepted? Through direct questions, open-ended questions, in-depth probing, or attentive listening?
+ What follow-up points would you like to establish during the discussion? Plan of action, meeting next week, interview with third party?
+ How do you plan to close the session? By summarizing the discussion or asking the other person to summarize?[3]

The Position Description as a Coaching Tool

To increase chances for getting off to the right start with key personnel, a formal up-front coaching policy can lay powerful groundwork for smoother running projects. Such coaching early in the project offers the possibility of adjusting individual managerial philosophies prior to the implementation stage, where major conflicts begin to appear. To emerge from the coaching series with a written agreement of understanding, use the position description as a base for negotiation. Project philosophies can be discussed while basic responsibilities and authority levels are adjusted.

The position description is a brief document that describes each individual's principal responsibilities, authority levels, and working relationships. Two pages of double-spaced text are usually sufficient to summarize these points. Existing position descriptions can be drawn on in preparing the draft, but for coaching purposes, it's better to start from scratch, letting the final form evolve during a series of give-and-take discussions. The person who is being coached should play a major role in preparing the document. The subordinate's involvement ensures commitment to the issues negotiated. A sample procedure for involving the subordinate follows:

1. Broach the subject in a chat, outlining the basic idea. If the other person isn't familiar with the position description concept, furnish sample descriptions. Suggest that the matter be given some thought and that a draft version be sent to you in the near future. (Allow some time for getting used to the idea.)
2. In the next session, give your comments on the draft and return it with your notes and observations. Discuss each point thoroughly during the session. Suggest that agreed-to changes be incorporated into a final document.
3. Limit the last session to making minor adjustments and sealing the deal with a handshake.

Through this procedure, a binding psychological contract is struck with the other person; in the process, some of the unknowns that frequently haunt working relationships later in the project are eliminated. A sample position description for the project manager of a construction project is shown in Figure 4–1.

Training Sessions

Training sessions represent a veritable "horn of plenty" of project blending agents. Various approaches can be pieced

Figure 4-1. Sample position description for a project manager.

Purpose: To implement the project within budget and according to project specifications, project schedule, and corporate policy and procedures.

Responsibilities:

- To determine jointly with the project sponsor and client representatives:
  - Project policy.
  - Basic organization.
  - Project procedures.
  - Key personnel requirements.
  - Special project requirements.

- To oversee implementation of project planning and control systems.

- To manage and coordinate:
  - Budget.
  - Schedule.
  - Project quality.
  - Engineering.
  - Procurement.
  - Construction.
  - Administrative services.
  - Job statements.
  - Project estimates.
  - Cost reports.
  - Correspondence.

- To oversee solicitation, evaluation, recommendation, award, and management of contracts.

- To hold staff meetings and project schedule reviews as needed.

- To report project progress, execution of work, and contract status to the project sponsor, client, and other interested parties.

Authority: The project manager has all authority necessary to carry out responsibilities provided actions do not violate:
- Local, state, or national laws.
- Generally accepted ethical practices.
- Corporate policy.
- Established project policy.

Working relationships: The project manager represents the company in dealing with the client and reports within the company to the project sponsor. Key personnel who report directly to the project manager include the business manager, project engineer, engineering manager, planning and control manager, procurement coordinator, and construction manager. The project manager receives staff assistance and advice from the home office and has line authority over all project personnel and a matrix relationship with home office departments.

together into multifaceted training programs. Some of the classic forms to choose from are lectures, round table discussions, and seminars.

Subject matter for these educational packages is abundant. For instance, the following behavior topics can be covered: interpersonal relations, conflict management, group dynamics, motivational techniques, team building, and effective communication practices. Management subjects include time management, managerial psychology, organizational development, delegation, "meeting management," and managerial assessment and diagnosis. Project topics such as the following can help tie management and behavioral themes into a harmonious form: the project plan, planning and scheduling, project reviews, costing systems, project engineering, design "freeze," fast tracking, kick-off meetings, start-up procedures, and subcontract management. The right combination of training approaches, using behavior, management, and project topics, is sure to give a boost to the overall effort.

Lectures

The lecture has a one-way characteristic that facilitates cramming large amounts of information into a small time frame. Lectures given by experts can bring top-quality information to the project arena. When the speaker is well known, the lecture will be sure to stimulate special interest.

The unidirectional, nonparticipative nature of a speech can limit its effectiveness. Information is often not retained by audience members. The lecturer proceeds without the benefit of feedback to discover if the message is being effectively received. Even the customary question-and-answer session at the end of a presentation doesn't substantially increase the lecture's effectiveness.

In spite of these drawbacks, however, there is no reason to scratch lectures from the roster of motivation tools. A well-timed speech can raise a topic that project team members need to be aware of. When workers react negatively to the idea of participating in more ambitious training schemes, the lecture is an acceptable alternative.

Lecture subjects likely to attract attention include: (1) living with project conflict, (2) project team-building techniques, (3) project planning and control, (4) time-management techniques for key project personnel, (5) project management overview, and (6) organizational approaches to project management. Qualified lecturers can be chosen from such organizations as the National Association of Speakers, the Project Management Institute, INTERNET-International Management Systems Associations, and Toastmaster Clubs. Authors of professional literature are also possible sources. It's important to remember, however, that the greatest expert in the field isn't always a good speaker, so great care should be taken in selecting both topics and lecturers.

While a lecture alone is rarely enough to spark project synergy, it is a valuable ingredient. When combined with other management tools, it can set off a reaction leading to the proper project blend. In scheduling project lectures, follow these guidelines:

1. Choose an appealing subject. Verbally poll co-workers or circulate questionnaires within the project group to get feedback on the topic.
2. Use speakers who are recognized experts with proven track records at the podium.
3. To arouse interest, distribute sample literature, such as a copy of a magazine article or a brief summary, several days prior to the lecture.
4. Make a checklist of all logistic points, including physical installations and audiovisual requirements.
5. At the lecture, maintain an objective focus by following this straightforward sequence:
   ♦ Brief introduction of the speaker
   ♦ Speaker's presentation
   ♦ Question-and-answer period
   ♦ Acknowledgments and closing remarks

Round Table Discussions

Round table discussions provide another approach for giving a motivational shot in the arm to the project team. At the same time, they provide an opportunity for obtaining feedback to plan more in-depth training programs. Round tables differ from lectures in that outside experts are not involved. The idea is to break ground for open-forum debates on pertinent project subjects, giving participants a chance to air views and present their opinions and ideas frankly. The goal is to establish a consensus.

Round tables feature overview discussions about a project's philosophy, goals, and criteria, as opposed to discussions designed to identify solutions to specific problems. For instance, a theme of "Project Planning: Alternative Approaches" sets the stage for a better round table than does "Which Software Is Most Appropriate for This Project's Scheduling System?" The first theme addresses broad questions that lurk *behind* specific issues. A more expansive theme lets participants educate one another as to how the subject under discussion fits into the overall picture. Specific topics are more appropriately solved in the project's operational arena.

Round table themes must be of a broad nature, yet they must be specific enough to generate healthy cross-fire between general concepts and nitty-gritty applications. Avoid themes that are too broad to tie into project realities or so specific that they invade the territory of day-to-day problem solving.

Here are some examples of subjects appropriate for the round table approach:

- Project phases and the shifting focus of project management.
- Project planning: macro and detailed.
- Subcontracting from start to finish.
- Shifting behavioral gears in project management.
- Controlling project design.
- Administrative support: how it fits in.

- The realities of fast tracking.
- Procurement interfacing.
- The subtleties of a matrix organization.

This list provides classic project topics rich in contrast and opposing views. However, the topics must be customized to meet the specific needs of each unique project.

Round tables are comparatively easy to organize, and successful ones can be developed by a simple planning process. Be sure to consider the following questions:

- What is the theme of the round table?
- What is the objective of the round table? Is it a one-time get-together, part of a team-building series, an opportunity for certain team members to contribute?
- What will be used as a basis for the discussion? Will it be a case study, a professional paper, experiences on prior projects?
- When will the round table be held? What time of year, phase of the project, day of the week, time of day?
- Where will the event be held? In a project meeting room, hotel, or special facilities?
- Who will be the session moderator? Should you use a member of the project team, the project manager, or an invited guest?
- Who will make the opening remarks at the session? A special dignitary, the project director, or the session moderator?
- Who will be the "theme speaker," giving a brief overview of the subject to set the tone for discussion (project team member or project manager)?
- Who will be the program coordinator—the person responsible for preparation and follow-through of event activities?
- How will the session be conducted? Should you arrange for formal, uninterrupted presentations or should you encourage those with comments to speak up on the spur of the moment?

+ How many people should participate?
+ How can the participants be "primed" ahead of time to ensure active participation in discussions? Should you distribute materials, conduct personal interviews, or prepare written surveys?
+ How long will the session last?

To obtain the best results, three points are of particular significance: (1) prior priming of the participants with literature, pre-event interviews, or questionnaires, (2) quality of the theme (both the subject and handouts), and (3) quality of the keynote or opening presentation. If these items receive careful attention, the event will be successful, even if slip-ups occur in other areas. On the other hand, if the rest of the preparations come through with Grand Prix-like precision, but the "priming," theme material, and opening delivery are below standard, the occasion risks being chalked up as a giant time-waster.

Seminars

Seminars or workshops combine the information content of the lecture with the opportunities for participation offered by the round table. In the seminar, information is dispensed in smaller doses interspersed with group discussions and debates. Seminars are established around a larger time frame than lectures or round table discussions. Two- to three-day seminars are the most popular, but one-day events are acceptable and five-day seminars are right for a more in-depth coverage.

A seminar is a stage for the discussion of any selected theme; it can be organized in a number of ways. Various teaching methods can be used throughout the event to give it variety while simultaneously providing the repetition needed to get across the basic points. The following tools and resources can be used in the seminar format: videotapes, films, slides, overhead projections, case studies, class lectures, group discussions, group problem solving, simulations and play acting, surveying, group self-analysis, and games.

Each project situation calls for a tailored training approach to meet the special needs of the audience at hand. Each project has its own special gaps, which call for corrective training emphasis. In dealing with a particular weak point, however, don't reinvent the wheel. Virtually all managerial and project subjects have been addressed at some time, either in public seminars or during other projects. Excellent sources for finding out about these topics and for locating specific training ideas are professional associations such as the Project Management Institute, INTERNET, and the American Association of Cost Engineers.

Stimulating seminars are often created by combining lecture presentations, case studies, group debates, project games, and training exercises. Each seminar should be conducted by a competent moderator. If an in-house specialist with a proven track record in conducting seminars is available, then the problem of selecting a moderator is solved. Otherwise, a specialist should be brought in to work out details with an in-house coordinator prior to handing over the baton for leading the event. Here's a list of points for moderators and coordinators to consider when organizing a seminar:

- Is the seminar supported by the people who matter, such as key personnel, client representatives, and upper management? If it's not, seminar "marketing" efforts need to be activated.
- Has the seminar's theme been customized for the project, using information from written or verbal canvassing or special studies?
- Who will conduct the seminar? The proposed moderator should be knowledgeable about the subject and experienced in conducting seminars.
- Has provision been made for coordinating logistics (locale, audiovisuals, support materials and equipment, special requirements, transportation, meals, awards, and final evaluations)?

Formal Team-Building Programs

Of the approaches aimed at heightening project synergy, the formal team-building program is apt to bring the best results. This type of program is head-and-shoulders above other team-building overtures because: (1) the longer program duration provides a greater opportunity for retention of concepts as they are reworked throughout the program, (2) on-the-job experimentation of the concepts provides timely feedback while the course goes on, (3) in-depth treatment can be given to subjects, and (4) enough time is available to build a strong consensus among participants.

However, ambitious programs aimed at generating subjective and unmeasurable results can come under fire. Common reactions to a major program include: "Isn't project synergy supposed to happen naturally? I thought that's why we hired the project manager and all his high-priced cohorts." "That type of program is not in the budget." "Couldn't we trim it down so it wouldn't take up so much time?" Countless projects have been successfully completed without the help of formal team-building efforts. And while the results of such programs are nearly impossible to quantify, the time and cost of putting them on are easily assessed. Thus, pushing for a large-scale team-building program is bound to draw a certain amount of flack.

Although the far-reaching team program can have great positive impact on the project, it is certainly not a panacea for project woes; in fact, in many cases it is not even appropriate. Some projects stand out as obvious candidates for ambitious training programs; others are better dealt with by less formal approaches. Projects that stand to gain most from a broad training program are those that accumulate some of the following characteristics: They are long running, bring together numerous high-caliber people who have not worked together previously, are part of a series of new projects, have large budgets, require interaction involving different cultural groups, and require interaction involving sharply different technologies. Projects best left to less ambitious training approaches are those that have sharply restricted budgets, are on short time schedules, have well-integrated technologies, and have limited cultural-integration needs.

A formal team-building program might require from 50 to 100 hours, spread across a comfortable time frame. An intensive one-day course could be right for a given project, whereas for others a longer course conducted over several months might be best. Barring special circumstances, however, a range of six to ten weeks is preferred. Programs crammed into shorter periods run the risk of over-saturation, while course-work distributed over many months may run out of gas.

An alternative approach to custom-building a formal program is to add extra hours to the participative segments of a broad-based seminar and integrate the theme into the program objectives. A formal program differs from a seminar mainly in the extent of in-depth treatment possible in a formal program, which has a greater number of hours.

A formal program calls for more preparation and follow-through than other team-building efforts. It's also important to plan well ahead of time to sell the idea, to make sure funds are available, to work out details of the program, and to follow up as the course goes on.

Marketing Approaches to Blending the Project

"I don't have time to take off two days for chitchatting," said a disgruntled construction superintendent.

"I'm looking forward to the project seminar so we can get ourselves organized," commented a hopeful contracts manager.

These contrasting views spotlight typical diverging expectations among participants in training or motivation programs. Some may see training efforts as giant time-wasters; others count on the seminar to place the project on an even keel and guarantee future smooth sailing; still others approach training activities with optimistic ambivalence, which is characterized by a balance of both hopes and doubts.

To establish what the programmed event will and will not do, basic marketing is required. Depending on the level of resistance that exists, the marketing effort may need to be intensified to obtain program approval. Here are some guidelines that can be used to help raise the level of interest of those involved or potentially involved:

+ Plant the seed: circulate a pamphlet, summary sheet, or other visual tool to create awareness.
+ Start off by mentioning the concept casually, without trying to force approval or commitment.
+ Distribute a summarized view of the training approach; add references or literature that support the training idea.
+ Involve superiors in specifics; try to capture ideas to include in the program.
+ Incorporate suggestions and submit the summary again, this time asking for a go-ahead.

Conclusions

The proper project blend can be reached by accentuating team-building efforts. Mixing together the right ingredients through such programs contributes substantially toward reaching the state of "project integration." Ways for fostering project integration include: setting examples, coaching, conducting training sessions, and using formal team-building approaches. All of these efforts require a marketing effort to ensure that key decision makers will approve the programs. For the project management recipe to work, artful project blending is a must.

References

1. Erasmus H. Kloman, *Unmanned Space Project Management—Surveyor and Lunar Orbiter* (report pre-

pared by the National Academy of Public Administration, sponsored by the National Aeronautics and
Space Administration, Washington, D.C.: U.S. Government Printing Office, 1972), p. 14.

2. Kahlil Gibran, *The Prophet* (New York: Alfred A.
Knopf, 1923), p. 56.

3. Adapted from R. E. Lefton, V. R. Buzzotta, and Mannie
Sherberg, *Dimensional Management Strategies* (St.
Louis: Psychological Associates, 1978).

Chapter 5

Planning and Strategy in Project Management

My interest is in the future because I'm going to spend the rest of my life there.

C. Kettering

The Planning Function

The underlying truth of Murphy's Law, which, in its simplest form, says, "If anything can go wrong, it will," is attested to by its popularity and universal acceptance. Murphy's Law has two aspects that may help account for its popularity. When things regularly go wrong, there's some solace in knowing that a "law" said it was bound to happen anyway. One can assume that a better approach or ingenious solution wouldn't have helped, because the outcome is an unfortunate, preordained stroke of fate. This view of Murphy's Law might be called the reactive side. Seen proactively, however, Murphy's Law clearly sheds light on the need to avoid potential problems. "If anything *can* go wrong. . ." alerts us to the importance of anticipating and preventing problems, which is the theme of this chapter. The Law implies that problems may be avoided by making sure things *can't* go wrong. While no solution is foolproof, the probability of failure can be reduced through adequate planning, scheduling, and controlling.

If you don't know where you're going, how are you going to get there? Knowing your destination before starting a journey is like opening your mouth before taking a drink of coffee, or removing your shoes before taking off your socks. It's so fundamental that it can hardly be questioned. Knowing where you're going involves mapping out the journey before it begins. Planning involves thinking through the trip ahead of time in an effort to steer clear of potential problems.

Management experts agree that planning should be a major part of a manager's job, but there is no consensus about what actually constitutes the planning task. Cleland and King's definition, however, which describes planning as "the activities which are variously referred to as goal setting, policy making, strategic planning, and strategic decision making,"[1] is particularly consistent with the view used in this chapter.

What function does project planning serve? What is it supposed to accomplish? Why should project teams go through time-consuming planning steps? Here are some classic responses in support of the planning function:

+ The critical path is determined.
+ Activity interfaces are defined.
+ Resources are gauged.
+ Schedules are determined.
+ Costs are related to schedule.
+ Control systems are interfaced with plans.

These reasons justify the respected position of the planning function in large, intricate projects. Planning produces a blueprint of the activities required for performing the job. If the plan is a sound one and is closely followed, the

probability of successfully completing the project is substantially improved.

Planning vs. the Plan

Planning is a means for getting things done, and not an end;
the process of planning is as important as the plan itself.
An effective planning process not only establishes what is
to be done during the project's implementation, but also
smooths the way for making it happen. It sparks an awareness
of the project's needs and at the same time paves the way
for meeting those needs. The synergistic or multiplier effect
created by participative planning corresponds to that generated by the consensus approach to decision making.

If planning is perceived as a vehicle for getting people
to cooperate to meet goals, the process of planning takes on
an expanded dimension. When performed jointly, planning
clears communication channels and obliges participants to
"sign on." The communication and commitment fostered
during the participative planning phase carry through to
implementation. In other words, when plans are drawn up
by those who will be carrying them out, levels of performance are raised as participants work on tasks to which
they have previously committed themselves. Dynamic interaction among participants during planning sets the stage
for enhancing synergy; a lack of interaction may lead to
plans being ignored, misinterpreted, or sabotaged. Thus an
effective planning process causes:

- A common basis for project communications to be
  established
- Project personnel to become more involved and committed

Management's participation in the planning process is
necessary—high-level personnel should be involved in planning the activities for which they are ultimately accountable.

High-level participation helps cut down on the productivity loss that results when "planners plan and doers do." When planning and implementation roles are not performed by the same people, the following problems or conditions can arise:

- Sense of accomplishment is less when executing someone else's plan.
- There is less tendency to try to confirm the validity of another's plan by executing it successfully—less confidence that it can be done.
- There is less commitment to see that the plan works well.
- There is less flexibility and less room for modification and initiative to make improvements in an assigned plan.
- There is less understanding of an assigned plan.
- Human resources are not so well utilized.
- There are more communications problems and consequent errors and distortions in following instructions.
- There are competitive feelings aroused between planners and doers, to such an extent that it appears as if the former "win" and the latter "lose."[2]

Behavioral problems such as lack of commitment, misunderstanding, and unclear communication permeate the list. In fact, all the above are behavioral problems. The best reason for going through the awkward, time-consuming planning process is to work on the behavioral side of project management.

In contrast with a behavior-oriented participative approach, a planning philosophy called technocratic planning is embraced by some project managers. In the technocratic school, participants are concerned with the plan itself. Implementation is a task for *others* who will perform the work. Emphasis is placed on coming up with the right answer. Planning is done by planners, with little help from the doers responsible for project implementation.

These two apparently conflicting schools are actually complementary approaches. Just as two hands rubbed together generate warmth and energy, joint concern for the plan itself (technocratic planning) and optimization of the behavioral benefits of the process (people-oriented planning) will yield both sound plans and commitment to perform.

Personal Approaches to Planning

How project managers and project team members go about planning hinges largely on their personal planning postures. Here are some differing planning poses:

- *Intuitive-anticipatory planning:* Mapping out schemes for performing future activities on the basis of insights or "gut feelings."
- *Formal strategic planning:* Plotting a program according to fixed procedures using a detailed written form.
- *Informal day-to-day problem resolution:* Short-term planning in which problems are evaluated as they occur.
- *Entrepreneurial opportunistic planning:* Focuses on finding and exploiting opportunities that involve uncertainty and risk.
- *Incremental muddling-through:* A wait-and-see, reactive approach to planning geared toward adjusting existing imperfections rather than charting strategies for meeting new goals.
- *Adaptive approach:* Starting from a strategic stance that is modified by successive decisions. The basic strategy is thus refined and adjusted as events evolve.[3]

In project work as in other kinds of business, no single planning process is used alone. One philosophy may be predominant, yet others exist among individuals and subgroups. A "philosophy gap" represents a major planning difficulty. Some managers prefer intuitive planning as a way to organize thoughts for the future. Others would not consider using anything short of a detailed written plan. And, to compound the problem, ". . . most people do not like to plan openly in concert with others. It is difficult creative work. It is revealing, and most people don't like to lay their technical or business soul bare to be seen and abused by others."[4]

Gathering and Evaluating Information

How managers' minds assimilate and organize information, and how they evaluate it, has a strong influence on planning. There are two types of thought processes used in information gathering: the preceptive and the receptive.[5] In a preceptive approach, the gatherer looks for a way to relate the data to existing mental concepts, patterns, or systems. Preceptive planners scan data in search of patterns; receptive planners are detail-oriented—they are concerned with the information itself and tend to withhold judgment until the facts have been fully examined.

Information is also evaluated in two distinct ways: intuitively or systematically. Intuitive thinkers examine material in an unstructured manner, searching constantly for alternative solutions, avoiding commitment until the last minute. Systematic thinkers study situations in an organized, logical manner. Alternatives are rationally screened and conclusions are defended based on the appropriateness of the process used.

People's thinking processes affect how they go about planning. Preceptive information gatherers and intuitive thinkers tend to conduct informal, unstructured planning and avoid more formal approaches. Receptive gatherers and systematic evaluators, on the other hand, tend to conduct planning efforts on a logical procedural basis, aiming for a refined formal document as the final product.

Which approach is best? It depends. According to studies of brain function, the looser, preceptive-intuitive mode corresponds to thinking patterns that occur on the right side of the brain, which houses emotions and abilities for si-

multaneously processing and randomly evaluating information. That approach is more appropriate for abstract, confusing, or creative challenges.[6] Systematic or logical thinking
takes place on the brain's left side, where information is
processed in a sequential and orderly way. This thinking
pattern is best for data-heavy situations that call for a structured analysis.

Studies have concluded that the thinking patterns of
good managers correspond to the right side of the brain,
while effective planners think on the left side.[7] This broad
generalization may be applicable for upper-echelon managers
who deal exclusively with fact-scarce policy issues and for
planners assigned to detailed planning efforts, but for those
managers and planners who work in the interface between
management and planning, an ability to cross over between
intuitive and systematic thinking is a must. For example,
in project work an overall project plan or an integration
plan requires a heavy dose of management intuition, yet
systematic thinking is also helpful. Detailing a work breakdown structure, on the other hand, is systematic in nature,
but intuitive thinking can be an asset. Planning is generally
enhanced by a combination of the two styles, with relative
emphasis shifted toward the intuitive mode when dealing
with unquantifiable abstract items, and toward the systematic approach when procedure and detail are indicated.

The Project Plan—Or, First Things First

A project plan supported by key project members and others
who influence project destiny is fundamental for achieving
project goals. This overall game plan should be presented
in a simple document that includes project policies, philosophies, guidelines, responsibilities, and major milestone
events. It provides a framework for the more detailed plans
that are developed subsequently, as a function of the overall
plan.

The project plan corresponds to corporate strategic planning in that it represents fundamental governing policies and philosophies. In the academic world, the procedure is sometimes referred to as "mapping." In project management literature, "project plan" is most commonly used. "Project policies" also describes these fundamental project cornerstones. The label given to the planning umbrella, however, is irrelevant. It is important that it be prepared, preferably in a collective form, by people who will exert strong influence on the project as it progresses.

The idea of the overall plan is to create a common framework upon which to hang the details. In the early project stages, the plan aggregates project policies, which are then used to outline detailed plans. Once the cornerstones are set in place, implementation becomes straightforward—if the participating parties have committed themselves to the general policies fixed in the plan.

What Is a Project Plan Made of?

As projects are one-of-a-kind ventures, project plans are also unique. They must be tailored to the needs of specific projects. The nature of projects is so varied that using a canned planning approach is simply impractical. Consider the contrast, for instance, between the characteristics of a construction project like the Alaskan pipeline and a ship-building project. Major capital ventures such as the pipeline project are fraught with logistical nightmares, huge capital outlays, and major technological barriers, all of which must be put into a coherent strategic plan. A ship-building project, however, may be only one of several ongoing projects in a shipyard that faces multiresource and multiproject planning problems. Several separate projects may have to share common resources. Because of these differences, highly structured planning techniques rarely have the flexibility required to span the planning gap between different types of projects. Thus, there is no formula for cranking out a project plan. It can't be preprogrammed or simply drawn from similar plans elaborated for other projects.

However, there are major checkpoints that should be considered in preparing the plan. To get an initial grasp on the project, the following steps are required:

1. Fix the objectives.
2. Examine the project environment.
3. Define the scope of the work.
4. Size up the types of relationships needed to effectively manage the project.

These items serve as a basis for taking initial action-related steps. To move from the broad overview to specifics, an evaluation of the systems to be applied is also fundamental. Once this groundwork has been laid, the project plan should be capped off with an "initial action plan" that will set the project into motion.

Project plans can be prepared in varying levels of detail. In contrast to the four simple checkpoints given in the previous text, Cleland and King itemize major project planning topics as follows:

- Project summary
- Project schedules
- Project management
- Market intelligence
- Operational concept
- Acquisition
- Facility support
- Logistical requirements
- Manpower and organization
- Executive development and personnel training
- Financial support
- Project requirements
- General information
- Proprietary information[8]

This checklist can also be used as a basis for a more detailed project plan.

Here's yet another version of an integrated planning process with a distinctly in-depth focus that involves the following detailed steps.

- *Mission statement:* a written statement describing the specific product or result that the management sponsor expects
- *Milestones:* the significant events necessary to the project's success
- *Work breakdown structure (WBS):* the project broken down into work packages
- *Organizational responsibility:* a consensus on the assignment of responsibilities for the work in the WBS
- *Activity cards:* specific activities and estimates of the resources necessary for their completion
- *Precedence diagram:* the relationships among project activities and milestones
- *Network schedule:* the precedence diagram used to prepare a schedule
- *Planning and controlling costs:* financial support of the project; establishing appropriate measures of financial performance
- *Management review and approval:* the plan then becoming the project's "charter"[9]

In some cases, the detail called for in the foregoing list might set back the timely release of the plan. If, however, resources, availability of information, and organization culture permit, a comprehensive approach can occur within a reasonable time frame. If conditions are not as favorable, however, an abbreviated version may be necessary so that the plan can be issued in time. Whatever details are lacking can be added later in accordance with a schedule proposed in the abbreviated plan.

Underlying Principles

The type of strategic project planning discussed above is actually broad-brush planning designed to deal with major issues and policies. It differs sharply from the work performed by the planning department of staff groups. Strategic project planning is performed by a group that works toward reducing project vagaries by compartmentalizing tasks, fixing time frames, and setting down policies regarding systems and implementation criteria.

Basic beliefs underlie the preparation of a strategic project plan. A planning culture is critical for the success of organizational strategic planning. If participants in the planning scheme are attuned to the strategic planning concept, the process can be fruitful. Research has led to the following list of principles underlying the preparation of strategic project plans:

- Professional planners can facilitate a planning process, but they cannot themselves do the planning.
- Planning activities should be performed by the managers who will ultimately be responsible for the implementation of the plans.
- Creative planning is inherently a group activity, since it must involve many different subunits of the organization and many different varieties of expertise.
- Strategic planning involves much more than numerical extrapolations of trends; it involves the final selection of strategic alternatives as well.
- The strategic planning involvement of managers must be broader than that usually achieved in a "management by objectives" framework.
- Managers must be motivated to spend time on strategic planning through a formalized system which permits their contribution to the planning process to be assessed.
- The planning process must provide for the development of relevant data bases—qualitative as well as quantitative—which facilitate the definition and evaluation of strategic alternatives.[10]

The points listed imply that strategic planning is an exercise in creative managerial design performed by a group of "implementers." Assisted by planners, this group of "doers" filters both qualitative and quantitative data to carry out the highly significant planning mission of defining and evaluating strategic alternatives.

Managers rather than planners are needed in the strategic planning process. If managers play a passive role in planning, the final plan will reflect the values of the planning technicians as opposed to those of managers. Since project success calls for commitment to completing the work outlined in project plans, major involvement is also required by key managers.

Planning, Scheduling, and Controlling

Plans determine what is to be done, establish the sequence of activities, and provide estimates of the time required for each activity. In the case of budgets, plans also spell out how much is to be spent on each activity. Schedules provide specific calendar dates for completion of activities and are used to monitor a project's progress. The control function consists of comparing actual performance with plans and schedules. In the case of cost control, it involves comparing actual costs and cost-to-completion estimates with original budget figures.

Plans cannot be automated. They can be prepared only by people, using judgment and prior experience. (Historical data can be retrieved and used as reference.) The scheduling task, however, can be supported by networking and data-processing techniques that speed up critical path calculations and provide timely data for weighing alternatives, evaluating resources, and establishing priorities. Cost control operations can also be accelerated by computerized techniques. The basic techniques used in preparing detailed plans, schedules, and controls for projects include: (1) the work breakdown structure, (2) Gantt charts, (3) milestone dates, (4) S-curves, (5) networking, (6) project procedures, and (7) cost controls. These methods are briefly described in Chapter 2.

Conclusion

The potential of project planning corresponds to that of an artist facing a blank canvas perched on a studio easel. With paints, brushes, and inspiration, the painter can make virtually any image appear on the canvas. A similar truth holds for planning projects. With skillful and imaginative planning, the project team can map out the project's format and destiny. Through the planning process, organizations can be changed and adjusted, philosophies formed, teams built, and projects accelerated or slowed down.

Effective project planning, however, is not limited to putting down ideas and lines on paper. To a greater or lesser extent, it requires a participative approach so that those who perform the tasks take on a commitment to perform the work planned. If the participative approach results in a general consensus, the subsequent implementation is greatly facilitated. If, however, plans are laid down by a restricted group and carried out by others, heavy management bridging and strong control tactics may be required to get the job done.

Project planning must start by tackling major project management issues and progressively moving down the scale to the details. The project plan encompasses major project issues and includes goals and milestones for completing other significant project management actions at later dates. The project plan acts as a tall-standing beacon for guiding the project through sometimes treacherous waters. Without such a guide, projects are almost surely doomed to face repeated crises—which are likely to occur even if minutely detailed implementation plans are developed. Crises cannot be avoided, or even diminished, if detailed plans leapfrog ahead of broad project plans. Project details must be subordinate to, and coherent with, the overall project plan.

References

1. David I. Cleland and William R. King, *Systems Analysis and Project Management* (Tokyo: McGraw-Hill Kogakusha, Ltd., 1975), p. 9.

2. Bernard M. Bass, "When Planning for Others" (New York: Management Research Center, University of Rochester, 1969).
3. George A. Steiner, *Strategic Planning* (New York: The Free Press, 1979), pp. 111–113.
4. Russell D. Archibald, "Planning, Scheduling and Controlling the Efforts of Knowledge Workers," *Project Management Institute Proceedings* (Philadelphia, September 1969), p. 7.
5. James L. McKenney and Peter G. W. Keen, "How Managers' Minds Work," *Harvard Business Review* (May–June 1974), p. 80.
6. Steiner, *Strategic Planning*, pp. 116–117.
7. Henry Mintzberg, "Planning on the Left Side and Managing on the Right," *Harvard Business Review* (July–August 1976), pp. 49–58.
8. Cleland and King, *Systems Analysis*, pp. 371–372.
9. Frank Reynolds, "Management of Research Projects," *Project Management Institute Proceedings* (Toronto, October 1982), p. IV-E.6.
10. Cleland and King, *Systems Analysis*, p. 164.

Chapter 6

Organizing Projects

The design of a flexible, or any other kind of, organizational structure is part of what some call "social architecture."

Russell L. Ackoff

Structure and Flexibility

"What a bureaucracy. I can't get anything to move in this organization."

"You're lucky there's a bureaucracy to complain about— there isn't any organization on our project. I don't know where my job stops and another person's starts."

These views reflect opposing complaints about the structure of an organization. The first is a reaction to rigid structures, which funnel information along routes mapped out by flow diagrams and organization charts. The approach allows little flexibility for making expeditious project moves. The second complaint emanates from a less structured organization characterized by unclear levels of authority and responsibility. In this organization, flexibility is so great that work boundaries become blurry and the result may be a project that, like the proverbial cooking pot, may have too many cooks watching over it—or, conversely, none at all.

94

In designing organizations, project decision makers must create structures that will meet widely diverse project needs. If the structure is too rigid—or too loose—the organization may provoke reactions similar to those given in the opening dialog.

Simply drawing an organization chart falls far short of designing a project's organization. In addition to sketching out who reports to whom, the overall design should respond to the question, "How will the organization really work?" It must provide for effective interaction among all of the project's players.

An organization's purpose is to facilitate the interaction of people to achieve goals. Jay W. Lorsch says that "the design of the organization is composed of the structure, rewards, and measurement practices intended to direct members' behavior toward the organization's goals." He goes on to give the following interpretation of managers' goals in designing organizations:

- To create an organization design which provides a permanent setting in which managers can influence individuals to do their particular job.
- To achieve the pattern of collaborative effort among individual employees, which is necessary for successful operations.
- To create an organization which is cost effective; that is, one which not only achieves the first two goals, but does so with a minimum of duplication of effort, payroll costs, etc.[1]

A structure that fosters human interaction, that minimizes barriers to such interaction, is required in setting up project organizations. Creating an organization can be compared to designing the basic framework of a building. A building can be structured of steel, reinforced concrete, wood, or other material. It can be beefed up or trimmed down depending on the probability of exposure to earthquakes, wind, ice, and temperature fluctuations. The building should reflect a coherent architectural style and should be compatible with construction needs. Project structures can take on various forms, exemplified by functional, matrix, or task force organizations. They can be tightened or loosened according to their relative needs. Style is also an important design factor for managing organizations. The organization must be styled to fit the predominant traits of company culture as well as the personalities and preferences of key project figures. Just as in structural design, each organization must be designed to fit a specific set of conditions.

Three classic structures prevail in project work. Although subtle variations exist, the cornerstones of organization design are represented by the following forms:

1. *Functional or hierarchical organization.* Reportedly the most prevalent type of organization in the world, the hierarchical structure is pyramid-shaped, with stratified management levels subordinated by distinct horizontal tiers. Work activities are divided functionally by specialties and disciplines.

2. *Task force organization.* In the task force organization, human resources pooled for a project team are largely separated from other company personnel ties. Centralized project management directs the project efforts.

3. *Matrix or horizontal organization.* The matrix organization is a hybrid structure aimed at optimizing strengths and minimizing weaknesses of the functional and task force structures. It is a loose functional structure in which extended lateral mobility exists.

A properly designed organization can be hailed as a major contributor to project success. Establishing the structure itself is only part of designing the organization, but it is a crucial part. An organization structure performs the following key functions:

• When unveiled, after being molded to specific needs, it represents a psychological "kick off," indicating that the project can move ahead at an increased clip.

 ♦ It formally establishes relationships among project team
   members and others.
 ♦ It implicitly or explicitly maps out work activities.

Inadequate Forms of Organization Structure

One explanation for the apparent inadequacy of existing
structures is the dynamic nature of projects. As projects
move through their life cycles, the work itself changes. Initial
phases are characterized by reflective thinking, planning,
and preliminary organizing. Intermediate phases require a
hands-on, action-packed approach. And project termination
requires a "mop up" philosophy.

Given such dramatic changes in the nature of project
activities, it is reasonable that structures be adjusted, or
even radically changed, during the project. Modifying the
organization may mean more than changing the hierarchical
structure. It may include adapting management systems and
processes, altering informal relationships, and changing behavior patterns. Inadequate organizational structures may
reflect management's inability to adjust the organization's
structure to changing needs as the project progresses through
its life cycle. The blame for project failings, however, may
not rest solely with the organization's structure. Inattention
to or improper application of management fundamentals,
such as project strategy, planning and control, motivation
programs, and communications skills, can contribute to low
productivity or failure.

The key to successful organization design is understanding that most project interaction takes place through people,
not through systems or things. It's people who make the
organization go, and cause significant things to happen. A
project must be organized so as to optimize the human
interaction required to carry out the activities necessary to
meet final goals.

The Functional Organization

The hierarchy, or functional organization, is an outgrowth of the classic bureaucracy. Max Weber, the renowned champion of this management form, claimed that a bureaucracy is technically superior to all other forms of organization and indispensable for large, complex enterprises. The hierarchy strives to be rational, efficient, and professional by establishing fixed authority relationships and defined spheres of competence.

The term "bureaucracy" has fallen into disfavor, although it is synonymous with the terms "hierarchy" or "functional structure." "Bureaucracy" is associated with negative characteristics such as narrow-mindedness, duplication of effort, and nonsensical rules. Unfortunately, the modern-day functional structure itself carries with it a certain amount of ill fame, and is low on the list of favorites for project management.

Yet the functional organization is not without attributes, or it would not have remained so prevalent in business and government. It offers clearly defined authority, strong discipline, and a setting that breeds technical competence. For many ongoing organizations and some project situations, the functional organization is quite appropriate. The inflexibility of the hierarchy can be a virtue in certain situations.

In project management, however, where multidisciplined projects must be completed within limited time frames and within predetermined budgets, the functional organization is often inadequate. Multispecialty ventures call for a horizontal form of coordination—a characteristic very foreign to vertically oriented bureaucracies.

However, a lack of lateral flexibility doesn't mean that functional organizations are entirely useless for managing projects. Projects can be directed from a functional base using an approach that Steiner and Ryan call "influence project management." The project is monitored or expedited from a staff position that is closely associated with a high-level executive post (see Figure 6–1). The functional organization remains intact; the staff member, working through the "influence" of the general manager's position, obtains information and performs follow-up functions. If the approach doesn't work, the general manager can either take on the role of project manager or revise the organization structure of the project.

Task Force Organization

The task force organization form has been called "pure" project management. It is a team effort created specifically to accomplish the project's objective or mission. The project manager deals from a charter establishing strong authority. Within the task force the manager is unencumbered by functional strappings and assumes a position of prestige,

Figure 6-1. Function organization with "influence project management" position.

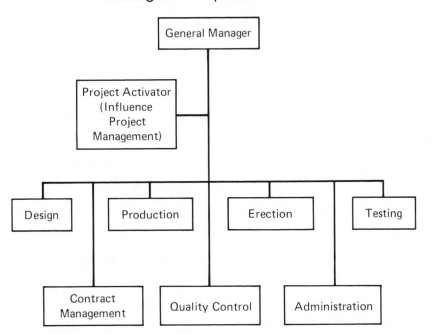

authority, and responsibility. Many major construction projects and special manufacturing projects, such as Lockheed Aircraft's "U-2" reconnaisance plane, built by the company's "Skunk Works" task force, qualify as project-oriented or task force organizations. A sample task force organization is shown in Figure 6–2.

The task force appears to many to be the ideal way to manage projects and is often referred to as the "projectized" form of organization. It is task-oriented, team-oriented, unhampered by restrictions imposed by the external organization, and buffered from external conflicts. These advantages make the task force a strong preference for many project managers.

Figure 6–2.   Task force organization for a manufacturing project.

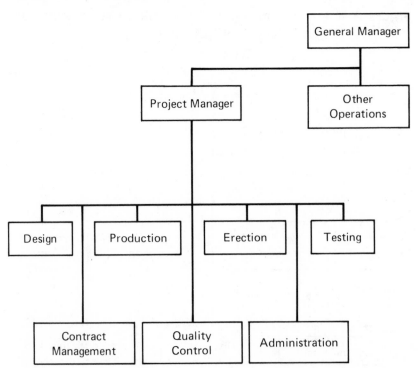

The task force carries with it, however, some significant disadvantages. Mobilization and demobilization of personnel are a major difficulty because the nature of the work is temporary. Where do the people come from? Where do they go once the project is completed? Technical expertise is difficult to maintain in projectized structures; qualified specialists may turn down temporary project assignments in favor of more permanent positions in functional settings. Also, because the costs of the task force organization are segregated, they may appear high in comparison with those of alternative organizational modes, where costs are included with overhead.

Both the functional organization and the task force organization have drawbacks when applied to project work. Attempts have been made to maximize the strong points of the two organization structures and minimize the weak ones. These efforts have resulted in the development of another type of organization—the controversial matrix organization.

Matrix Organization

Structures that are either purely functional or purely projectized are becoming relatively rare. More commonly found are organizations representing some type of matrix formation. While these organizations often carry strong functional or project overtones, the interconnecting web of relationships and responsibilities characteristic of matrix philosophy is always present. Figure 6–3 shows in a simple form how a typical matrix structure might exist for a manufacturing project. In this section, the advantages and disadvantages of the matrix as opposed to those of the functional and the projectized structures are discussed.[2]

The Matrix and the Camel

The camel is said to have been conceived by a committee whose initial task was to design a horse. The give-and-take

Figure 6-3. Matrix organization for a manufacturing project.

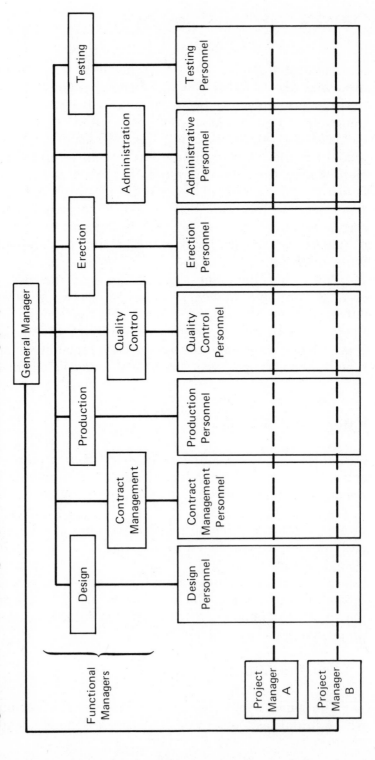

compromise of the committee members resulted in an awkward-looking and cumbersome creature that was nevertheless highly effective in the inhospitable desert environment for which it was created.

The matrix may be the organizational cousin of the camel. Surely the original goal was not the ambiguous, conflict-raising structure that finally evolved. Despite its ungainliness, the matrix model has proved to be effective in certain complex organizational environments that are perhaps as hostile as the camel's desert locale. Outside of their natural environments, both the camel and the matrix appear strange, clumsy, and very much out of place.

Matrix management is chock full of pros and cons. There are justifications for lauding the matrix as a solution for stamping out organizational blight. On the other hand, it can also be seen as a major root cause of corporate strife. Full-fledged horn-tooters for the matrix are relatively rare creatures, even though many support this management option as a solution that somehow meets a need, despite the drawbacks that emerge in day-to-day practice. The matrix can even be compared with marriage, which, in spite of known difficulties, has shown itself to be highly satisfactory when successful "consensus management" is practiced by husband and wife, who play the roles of "matrix managers" in the relationship.

The wide range of matrix combinations found in the business world reflects individual company peculiarities, cultural differences, and specific phases of organizational development. Some matrix organizations evolve naturally according to the type of work or the nature of the people involved. Other organizations turn to matrices when another approach being used becomes inadequate. Others may establish a matrix in an attempt to stay at the forefront of managerial advances in organizational development.

Changing over to a matrix system is not easy and is sometimes unfeasible. Even when the switch is made for the right reasons, no guarantee of success exists; as Drucker points out, the matrix is often "fiendishly difficult" to put into operation.[3]

What justifies the risk and potential pain of making such a change? Can the need for the shift be anticipated, or should circumstances come to a head to help spur the organizational evolution? Why will the new form be more effective than the old one? What are good reasons for not switching to a matrix system? In which situations would another structure be more appropriate? Should more traditional approaches be considered? The answers to these questions are explored in the following sections.

Advantages and Disadvantages of the Matrix Organization

Most organizations contain some of the ingredients needed for a matrix structure. Some organizations are loosely woven with informal channels of communication and participative decision-making processes. Others are tightly run operations in which information, people, and things move and interact only as determined by all-encompassing systems, standards, and procedures. Still other organizations are hybrid forms that contain the raw material for a smooth matrix operation—as well as a healthy array of stumbling blocks capable of making the whole thing inoperable.

Strong justification is required before putting any organization into the matrix mode and exposing it to the forces that result. Solid reasons must offset the risk and the natural human resistance that builds up against a structure so complex that it can be represented graphically only in an oversimplified form. There are apparent justifications for the matrix; however, on closer inspection, a good reason, standing alone or even in certain combinations with other reasons, may be insufficient to warrant the move.

Three basic conditions are required for the matrix organization to be effectively applied: (1) outside pressure for dual focus, (2) pressure for high information-processing capacity, and (3) pressure for shared resources. Where at least two of these conditions exist, the matrix structure should be considered an organizational solution; where none or only one of the conditions appears, establishing a matrix should be questioned.[4]

Outside pressure for a dual focus may represent a need to meet customer desires through a central spokesperson, even though the work is developed on a specialty basis within the company. The matrix can relieve the pressure for high information-processing capacity because, in terms of speed and agility, its horizontal and informal communication patterns give it a sizable advantage over other forms. The problem of pressure for shared resources can be met by the matrix, which is more resource-efficient than, say, a cluster of numerous independent project structures, which are bound to result in redundancies. The cumulative positive effect of these conditions may be sufficient to offset the difficulties of dealing with the conflict-prone, fuzzy organizational compromise called the matrix. However, each condition alone is not enough to justify abruptly switching to a matrix structure, although each carries an incentive to move in that direction.

Advantages of the Matrix

Let's listen to managers' comments about situations or problems in existing structures that indicate when a matrix may present a feasible solution.

 ◆ *"The way we're doing things isn't working."* Changing organizational strategy is always considered when things aren't going right. Yet the source of troubles may stem from a poor game plan, inadequate personnel, or substandard motivational programs. Before changing the organizational structure, evaluate the basics. Consider the conditions just discussed and ask: "Is there pressure for a dual focus?" "Is there a high information-processing requirement?" "Is there a need for shared resources?" If the answers to these questions are yes, then the matrix may indeed offer a chance for better performance.

 ◆ *"We're stuck in a giant bottleneck—things don't move."* The hierarchy or classic bureaucracy isn't known for solving problems at record-breaking speeds. While some functional organizations work better than others, all must cope with a cumbersome vertical communication system. The functional manager who strives to keep tabs on his area becomes a bottleneck, inadvertently slowing down communication. A solution is to stimulate horizontal communication practices. An emphasis on more open lateral channels results in a subtle power shift, with authority being siphoned from the functional manager's previously sovereign domain. This change, needed to break up the managerial bottleneck, represents a move toward a matrix system. In this sense, the matrix is an approach for loosening up the organization and helping things move along.

   ♦ *"We're not giving our customers what they need."* Many a customer or client who has tried to follow a design, system, or equipment package through a functional manufacturing organization knows the meaning of the expression "wild goose chase." Functional groups, set up along discipline lines, all know why their part of the project isn't further along. It's almost invariably because some other associated functional group hasn't completed its part of the job! The customer trying to follow up on the project ends up witnessing an in-house finger-pointing contest and often fails to get satisfactory responses to perfectly reasonable questions. The customer is unable to get an overview of what is happening and may feel the urge to cry out, "Who's in charge around this place anyhow? Can't anybody give me a straight answer?" By establishing a project coordinator, the vendor in a matrix format can centralize contacts with customers and consequently give coherent responses to customers' questions. The coordinator, motivated by the need to obtain information, helps move the project across interdisciplinary boundaries. For bettering the response to customer needs, the matrix offers a suitable solution.

   ♦ *"Our technical people don't have enough input."* A strong project-oriented organization may leave technical personnel out of the decision-making mainstream. If a well-balanced technical input is essential to the project, a shift toward the matrix helps adjust this "functional-to-project" ratio, giving the technical people more clout. Without such power, a functional manager in the aircraft industry might have reason to lament, "I feel confident the plane will be finished on time and within budget, but I don't think it will fly." The matrix gives all key participants, including technical people, room to maneuver within the project structure and opportunity to add their contribution. Such a contribution may be adding a simple finishing touch, or it may be waving a red flag and calling "back to the drawing board." The matrix is a way for keeping technical personnel from being "steam-rollered" by a management-heavy project group.

  ♦ *"There's dissatisfaction in the ranks."* Job satisfaction can be enriched by using a matrix, although the route is full of pitfalls. Take the case of the functional organization that has been frozen solid by bureaucracy. Project participants feel frustrated, until the structure is loosened up by using matrix relationships; this will soon encourage some positive project decisions. When structured for the right situation, the matrix can attenuate the types of disgruntlement that accompany a bureaucracy. If the cause for dissatisfaction is indeed an inadequate organizational structure, then the matrix should be considered as a possible solution.

  ♦ *"We need to reconcile time-consuming technical requirements with the need to get the job done on schedule."* The matrix is the epitome of compromise. It's a managerial solution that doesn't leave anyone turning backflips in glee. It attempts to be fair and to reach an acceptable midpoint. Fast-moving activities involving complex technology require technical watchdogs with enough sovereignty to keep the project sound. On the other hand, they also need goal-oriented "chargers" bent on meeting project milestones and budgets. The sometimes conflicting goals of developing the best technical solution and getting on with the job can be combined in a state of "unstable equilibrium" in the matrix organization. The matrix becomes a type of organized tug-of-war that, with able management, actually optimizes a project's resources and requirements.

♦ *"People are always writing letters and memos—we need a less formal approach."* Functional organizations are great at generating correspondence. Project organizations have also been known to spew reams of written material at clients. The matrix structure, however, tends to short circuit formal communication channels, putting in their place simple approaches such as telephone calls, problem-solving meetings, and face-to-face negotiations. Since many communication routes in the matrix are "dotted-line" or diagonal in nature, formal communications are not always practical. Also, since the matrix fosters consensus-type approaches, a verbal approach for getting to a decision is often more effective than going through formal channels.

♦ *"We're surrounded by red tape."* The matrix has a tendency to eliminate red tape. Excessive protocol, duplicated filing systems, and extensive rubber-stamping are pushed aside. The matrix gets people moving horizontally across the vertical organizational structure, searching objectively for solutions. This doesn't mean, however, that in a matrix people are necessarily swift and efficient. On the contrary, at times they can be exceedingly slow and cumbersome. The occasional slowness, however, stems from the complexity of interacting within a loose network rather than from a tight bureaucracy.

Disadvantages of the Matrix

Here are managers' comments that point out why changing to a matrix might not be advisable.

♦ *"The way we do it now is fine."* There is strong justification for maintaining the *status quo* when the present organization is, in fact, getting the job done. If straightforward approaches meet the project's needs, then there's no reason to switch to more complex forms. An organizational structure is, after all, a means for utilizing human and material resources to achieve goals. Indeed, the matrix is rarely adopted when other approaches are working reasonably well—it is often quite appropriately considered a last-ditch effort to use when all else fails. Even if the company's characteristics seem to call for a matrix framework, an organization that is operating satisfactorily should not switch to a matrix without considering the possibility that organizational effectiveness may actually be diminished rather than augmented.

♦ *"This is how we've always done it."* The fact that "it's always been done this way" may sound like an antiquated excuse for resisting organizational change. But it may be advisable to be cautious about implementing an organizational shake-up. Analyze the situation by asking: What are the consequences of making the move? Will employees welcome or resist the change? Will productivity drop? Will a morale problem arise? Will adaptation and training costs be prohibitive? On the other hand, what are the potential benefits of the change? Will profits increase? Will service improve? Is the change part of an overall shift in management philosophy that can occur gradually over time? "We've always done it this way" is surely not sufficient justification for resisting needed change; however, it serves a useful purpose for avoiding changes that occur simply for the sake of change.

♦ *"The matrix is too complex for us."* In a matrix, the consensus philosophy and the balance of power tend to force team members to feel their way along the foggy fringes of a project's interfaces in an attempt to push aside formal authority in favor of group synergy. If personnel targeted for working in the matrix are not prepared to operate in such undefined, nebulous situations, the confusion and frustration that result may be enough to make the matrix impractical. The ambiguous form of the matrix breeds conflict. Unless a comprehensive program is developed to train personnel to work within the matrix, the existing organizational structure might well be left as is.

♦ *"Figuring out who's in charge is too confusing."* The matrix can make communication from outside the organization simpler. Within the matrix, however, power relationships are often murky and fluctuating. At certain points in technically oriented projects, attention naturally shifts toward the technical centers of expertise. Yet not all shifts follow logical patterns. Informal "power surges" occur commonly in a matrix when certain individuals are extremely competent in specific areas that happen to be a transient focus of attention. Just as such power grows, it also wanes when people with other areas of expertise take priority. For Indians who are used to one chief, the matrix presents a confusing array of figures who at times pass the headdress from one to another, and on other occasions huddle in a powwow trying to make a joint decision. For people who are most comfortable with just one boss, a switch to the matrix may cause lower morale and a subsequent dip in productivity.

 ◆ *"Certain operations will be duplicated in a matrix arrangement."* The matrix has a built-in redundancy characteristic, which in the right situations yields dividends, but when applied out of context breeds internal head-butting and results in skyrocketing costs. For instance, if a systems manager in a remote international office is connected through a matrix to both the systems director at the home office and the general manager in the foreign country, the matrix relationship can bring benefits if: (1) complex technology prevails, (2) tie-ins with other company systems are required, and (3) the volume of work processed by the systems operations is large. On the other hand, if the systems are relatively simple and are restricted to isolated local use, participation of the home-office systems director might well be dispensed with. The organization might work better without a matrix arrangement.

 ◆ *"Responsibilities should be neatly outlined."* Matrix structures play havoc with definition of responsibilities. Rather than staking out discrete areas of "accountability," they tend to sire joint or group causes because of the integrated effort required. For personnel accustomed to well-drawn lines of action, the matrix must look like a toss-up between an organizational mess and a messed-up organization. The properly structured matrix creates an atmosphere in which everyone takes responsibility for final results. By the same token, the matrix structure can involve so many people that it dilutes responsibility to the point that no one feels responsible.

♦ *"The matrix breeds conflict."* High on the list of drawbacks is the matrix's propensity to breed conflict, even though all such conflict is not necessarily bad. The matrix provides an atmosphere of controlled conflict that spurs projects along. The conflict generated by a matrix can be compared with the intense diplomatic skirmishes that occur among international powers (controlled conflicts), which are much different from an all-out war (crisis). Conflict is part of the matrix game.

♦ *"Our functional department heads will never share their power base."* The switch from a functional organization to a balanced matrix can be traumatic for old-time department heads and even more traumatic for the company if the positions of the old-timers are well entrenched. Managers accustomed to strong power bases may be reluctant to give up the ego-satisfaction of centralized command. A successful move toward the matrix depends on artful training of functional managers and skillful interplay by the new project managers or coordinators. Unless steps are taken to set such a stage, resistance by functional managers (who probably control most of present operations) may be sufficient to destroy the effectiveness of a newly established matrix organization.

Types of Matrix Organizations

Either by design or as an outcome of the conflicting forces existing in the organization, the matrix tends to occur for substantial periods in one of the following matrix modes: (1) project matrix, (2) balanced matrix, or (3) functional matrix.

The *project matrix* adopts the matrix organizational format, yet is slanted toward task force philosophy. The project coordinators or managers assume more decision-making power than the corresponding functional managers. Schedule and cost goals are strongly emphasized. The project matrix is particularly applicable for activities requiring limited technical resources that can be drawn periodically from an existing "pool." It is also an appropriate structure for intermediate phases of some projects, for example, when a big project "push" is needed after technical parameters and basic concepts have been firmly set in place.

The *balanced matrix* distributes influence and decision-making power equally between functional discipline managers and project coordinators or managers. This is the classical matrix generally referred to in the literature. Decisions are negotiated among participants who are on an "even footing" with one another, resulting in ongoing trade-offs between quality-oriented goals (product, service, or project) and task-oriented goals (budget and schedule). Curiously, the degree of potential conflict tends to be greater in a balanced matrix than in the two other variations (project and functional matrix), because predominant power is more clearly defined in the latter two cases. The balanced matrix corresponds to an ongoing fencing match in which intense parrying for position may continue throughout the project.

The *functional matrix* is the opposite of the project matrix. The functional manager exerts a stronger influence on overall activities than the project coordinator or manager does. In the functional matrix, budget and achievement dates are subordinated to the greater concern for overall quality. This form sometimes evolves from a well-entrenched functional organization, where tradition and resistance to change prevent the structure from assuming a more balanced posture. The functional matrix is appropriate where cost and schedule performance are less important than overall quality. On fast-tracking, cost-sensitive projects, however, the technical matrix tends to lack goal-oriented managerial punch.

Figure 6–4 shows an organizational continuum demonstrating that "pure" project, matrix, and functional organizations represent discrete points among an infinite number of organizational variations. The shaded area represents the percentage of the project that is done by those outside the

Figure 6-4. Organizational continuum.

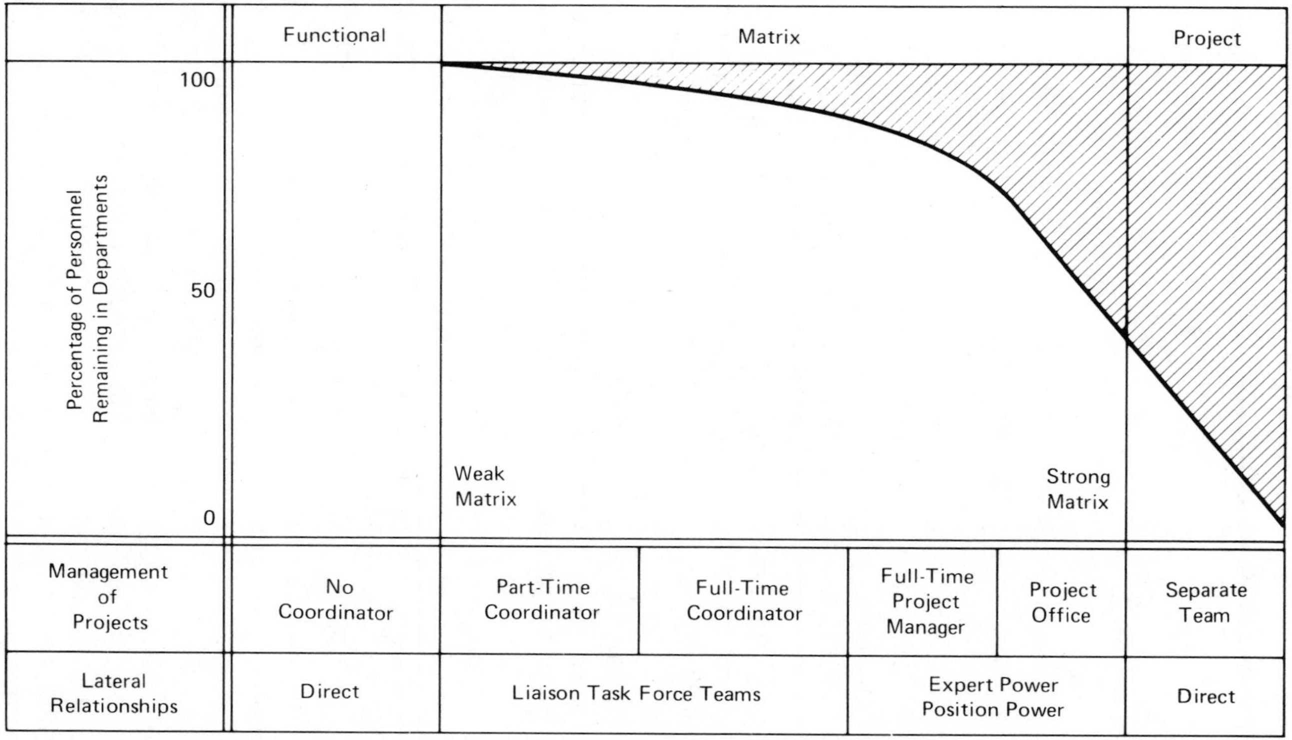

Percentage of Personnel Remaining in Departments	Functional	Matrix				Project
100		Weak Matrix			Strong Matrix	
50						
0						
Management of Projects	No Coordinator	Part-Time Coordinator	Full-Time Coordinator	Full-Time Project Manager	Project Office	Separate Team
		Liaison Task Force Teams		Expert Power Position Power		
Lateral Relationships	Direct					Direct

Source: J. N. Salapatas, "Project Management: How Much Is Enough?" *Project Management Institute Proceedings* (Los Angeles, October 1978), p. 11–D.7. Adapted by permission.

department. In reality, the specific forms discussed are merely reference points for relating to a large array of intermediate structures found in actual practice.

Conclusion

Three distinct structures serve as a basis for designing project-related organizations: functional, task force, and matrix. At one extreme is the "projectized" task force, and at the other is the functional structure. The matrix organization is a continuum inbetween, covering a range of variations.

Functional organizations are hierarchical, verticalized structures that establish clear lines of authority and foster competence within disciplinary specialties. Projectized structures use the task force team approach, marshaling necessary resources around a strong project manager in order to accomplish the project's goals. Matrix organizations result from attempts at making "the best of two worlds" by cross-breeding the functional and projectized forms. The matrix offspring combines the attributes of relative *efficiency* (through utilization of human resources) and *effectiveness* (through task-oriented coordination) with the not-so-desirable side effects of ambiguity and conflict. Each type of organizational structure meets project needs to greater or lesser degrees. The comparative performance of each as related to basic criteria is shown in Table 6-1, which is based on studies done in research and development (R&D) organizations.

Structuring an organization is only part of the job. Planning strategic management moves and providing for integration and active interfacing are part of the overall organization design and must specifically address the people side of project management. Designing a project organization, therefore, means both providing a basic organizational structure and complementing it with a strategic managerial philosophy sensitive to the behavioral needs of key project personnel.

Table 6-1. Comparative performance under project, matrix, and functional organizations for R&D projects.

Criteria	Project	Matrix	Functional
Achievement of due dates	Very good	Poor	Poor
Technical qualities	Poor	Good	Very good
Resource utilization (cost levels)	Poor	Good	Very good
Cost control	Very good	Good	Poor
Job satisfaction			
Specialists	Poor	Good	Very good
Non-specialists	Very good	Good	Poor
Client feedback and control	Very good	Good	Poor
Technical development of organization			
Unidisciplinary	Poor	Good	Very good
Multidisciplinary	Very good	Good	Poor
Conflicts	Low	High	Low

Source: Eduardo Vasconcellos and James Hemsley, "The Design of the Matrix Structure for R&D Organizations," *Project Management Institute Proceedings* (Boston, October 1981), p. 3. Adapted by permission.

References

1. Jay W. Lorsch, "A Note on Organizational Design," Harvard Business School, 9–476–094, Boston, 1975 (rev. 1977), pp. 1–2.
2. Text on matrix organization adapted from Paul C. Dinsmore, "Whys and Why-Nots of Matrix Management," in *Matrix Management Systems Handbook*, David I. Cleland, ed. (New York: Van Nostrand Reinhold, 1984), pp. 394–401, 405–406. Used by permission.
3. Peter F. Drucker, *Management Tasks, Responsibilities, Practices* (New York: Harper & Row, 1974), p. 598.
4. Stanley M. Davis and Paul R. Lawrence, *Matrix* (Reading, Mass.: Addison-Wesley, 1977), pp. 11–17.

Chapter 7

Project Interfacing

We love to overlook the boundaries which we
do not wish to pass.

Samuel Johnson

"Working the interfaces" is a major project management
function. An effectively interfaced project is a well-managed
project.

However, the sometimes-held notion that project management is synonymous with interfacing is incorrect; interface management addresses only boundary issues, or those
that are "floating" between defined areas of responsibility.
But a project's problems are not necessarily concentrated at
the boundaries. For instance, if consultants, contractors, or
functional departments operate at substandard levels, interfacing might not be enough to upgrade the quality of work.
The challenge in this case would be to stimulate improved
performance of independent project tasks within defined
areas, rather than to try to artfully blend activities together.
In fact, many of the nuts-and-bolts activities of project management tend to be performed within specific areas of responsibility. Those activities correspond to the "science" part
of project management, which includes such key elements

as (1) administration, (2) planning and scheduling, (3) cost control, and (4) technical tasks.

In "real life," however, a great deal does occur at the fringes of activity interface. The "art" of project management, those aspects that hinge on sensibility, feeling, and perception, take place there. Managerial actions that have lasting impact on the project tend to be born at the interfaces.

Interfacing Isn't Easy

Lackadaisical interfacing ultimately results in problems. Indeed, a casual interfacing stance is an open invitation to disaster. Unless the project team is particularly well equipped to stave off an onslaught of conflicts and trouble throughout the project, boundaries must be spanned proactively. Forward-looking interfacing offers a *preventive* approach for managing projects. Despite a proactive posture, however, some problems are inevitable, even in the most advanced interfacing scheme.

For example, a slip-up in the design/construction interface is exemplified by an overseas road project originally budgeted for $8 million and actually let for $7 million. But the 110 km gravel-surfaced road ended up costing $12 million. One reason: the zealous consultant "overwrote" the specifications. He went beyond the normal practice of presenting desired end results by explicitly describing the methods to be used by the contractor. The specifications determined the type of equipment for compacting the sandy clay base material and did not allow for the use of alternative machinery or methods. The contractor welcomed the opportunity to shift responsibility from his own shoulders to those of the consultant. Although he meticulously followed the specifications, the contractor never achieved the required compaction and consequently construction progress fell behind schedule. The contractor was finally allowed to use his own methods, but only after filing numerous claims of outside-imposed difficulties. Although he had operated with the best intentions, the consultant's interface error had exposed the project to major cost overruns.[1] Failure to fulfill "best intentions" can often be traced to subpar interfacing efforts.

Types of Interfacing

There are three distinct types of interfacing: personal, organizational, and systems.

♦ *Personal interfacing.* This type of interface is intrinsically related to human behavior. To deal effectively with the interface, behavioral barriers must be crossed and the boundaries between personal relationships must be considered. Coordinating these interfaces consists of closing gaps between people who must interrelate in order to do their jobs. This often involves finding ways of circumventing or eliminating the barriers put up by people who display behavior patterns that are in conflict with desired goals.

♦ *Organizational interfacing.* Interfacing between organizations is accomplished through people; therefore, personal interfacing is also implicit in organizational interfacing. Its primary aim is to span the gaps between organizational goals—companies, departments, and other groups often have partially conflicting objectives. In addition, organizational interfacing includes bridging gaps between clashing managerial styles, such as the autocratic versus the more open participative style.

♦ *Systems interfacing.* Systems interfaces include physical interconnections of parts that make up a whole system, as well as performance criteria required for subsystems to integrate with the overall system. This means, for example, that a motor shaft must be physically set and aligned to operate effectively. It also means that the motor must have the performance characteristics required to provide the necessary power to do its assigned task. Whereas systems interfaces are "nonpeople" in nature, it takes people-oriented management to ensure that systems interfaces are correctly handled.

Interfacing in Action

To design an organizational structure, activities must be segregated and responsibilities assigned. As a result of this segregation, responsibilities require interfacing with everything else that is part of the organizational structure. Interfacing is not always an easy task, however, especially in organizations that are relatively unstructured. In these cases, although certain activities may be considered "organized," the areas for interface may not be readily identifiable. Thus interfacing is strongly influenced by *how, to what extent,* and *under what conditions* people are actually clustered together in organizations.

There are various reasons for grouping people together. For example:

+ The nature of the work is such that activities naturally separate and repel one another.
+ A formal organizational structure has been established on the basis of an objective analysis of needs and prior experience.
+ Company culture determines the groups.
+ Prevailing philosophy of the project requires certain groups.

The interfacing implications differ for each organizational approach.

Interfacing Different Types of Activities

In capital construction projects, the working philosophy of each participating entity differs substantially from those of the other entities. Engineering design activities, for instance, tend to be based on systems. Air conditioning systems must be conceived and detailed as a coherent whole, as must fire-protection, potable water, and electro-mechanical control systems. The overriding concern in engineering design is to conceive and detail workable systems. Procurement, on the other hand, may be either item- or package-oriented. If all piping materials are to be purchased together to take advantage of large-volume discounts, itemized purchases can be made based on a composite of the components from the different piping systems. "Package purchasing," on the other hand, may coincide with the systems concept used in design. For instance, a turn-key air conditioning system could be one major procurement package. Construction philosophy is related predominantly to a physical area or facility. Turning over completed facilities is the construction group's goal, although each facility, building, or other distinct structure may be composed of systems common to the overall complex.

The project management team must recognize each group's philosophy and approach in order to mediate problems arising from conflicting work philosophies. Knowing that people see things in part according to the nature of the group activity being performed is fundamental to project interfacing.

Formal Organization Structure and Interfacing

Structural interfacing is determined by an organization's configuration. The spaces between the boxes on the project's organization chart must be spanned if the project's objectives are to be met. There are three types of structural interfacing:

1. *Vertical interfacing.* An up-and-down coordination of hierarchical relationships as established on the organization chart that involves activities such as training (downward interfacing) and "managing the client and/or the boss" (upward interfacing).
2. *Horizontal interfacing.* Horizontal or lateral interfacing consists of coordinating activities with peers. Formal authority is absent, although the relative power

base of one party may overshadow that of another. Behavioral skills play a particularly important role in horizontal interfacing.

3. *Diagonal interfacing.* Diagonal relationships are rarely shown on the organization charts. They include interplay with company officers from other areas (upward diagonal) and with subordinate groups in other areas and certain third parties such as contractors or project consultants (downward diagonal).

Predominant Culture and Interfacing

Interfacing problems must be dealt with sooner or later in any project. Interfacing modes may be developed early in the project's life in an attempt to smooth the way toward successful completion—or they may occur as needed during the project's life. If efforts to span gaps are slack in the beginning and ongoing phases, then the final stages will catch the brunt of accumulated "catch up" interfacing efforts.

Whether interfacing occurs early on, halfway through, or late in the project's life span, efforts must accommodate the overall culture that permeates the project. In the consensus-conscious Japanese management style, for instance, front-end interfacing usually results in early development of detailed plans designed to facilitate implementation and to maintain harmony (a state of importance in the Japanese culture). The fast-tracking American approach of charging onward before final details are worked out places a heavy interfacing burden on management during the implementation phase.

Overall Philosophy and Interfacing

The project's prevailing philosophy influences how things are done and who does them. If the project is to be performed by a turn-key contractor or vendor, then detailed interfacing will be done by the vendor in-house; the client's project management group is limited to macrointerfacing. If, however, a hands-on management philosophy prevails in which activities from numerous organizations and groups require detailed coordination, then the project management group will be called upon for constant and persistent interfacing.

Static and Dynamic Interfacing

Project interfaces can be divided into two categories, one representing needs for permanent interfacing and the other for transient coordination. These categories are called "static interfaces" and "dynamic interfaces."[2]

Static Project Interfacing

The need for static interfacing stems from the organizational structure itself. Such interfacing is carried on by permanent project groups, which undertake ongoing coordination efforts. These duties must be systematically performed in order to successfully conduct daily business and involve the following groups or people within the project:

- *Planning and control.* An independent group that is the hub of technical and performance interfacing, its responsibilities include the gathering, processing, and disseminating of information that others need to complete project tasks.
- *Project manager.* As the primary interfacer, the project manager is the focal point for a project's success. Major interfacing moves are generally instigated or actively supported by the project manager.
- *Functional groups.* Groups organized along discipline or specialty lines need constant interfacing. Engineering, logistics, procurement, and construction are interdependent, yet they have defined boundaries that must be crossed regularly throughout the project.
- *Subprojects.* In multiproject undertakings, ongoing interfacing is required between the central project group and the subprojects that constitute the overall complex.

Dynamic Project Interfacing

Dynamic interfaces are transient in nature and arise from technological, organizational, or schedule constraints. They vary appreciably from project to project. Dynamic interfacing poses several challenges, the first and greatest of which is to simply identify the need. Because dynamic interfacing needs are not constant—they vary in intensity over time—the requirements must be promptly detected in order to trigger the necessary managerial touches. Project interfacing calls for placing the right people in the right place at the right time. The third challenge involves focusing on each interfacing need for as long as required and then moving on to other demands.

Dynamic interfacing can be split into two categories: (1) process technology and (2) managerial. *Process technology dynamic interfacing* includes efforts to gain acceptance of project scope and basic engineering design and to accomplish design/manufacturing coordination, design/construction coordination, and plant start-up coordination. *Managerial dynamic interfacing* encompasses less technical yet equally important areas such as overall subcontracting policies, administrative procedures for letting major contracts, and the degree of fast tracking involved in project phases.

Principles of Managing Project Interfaces

To properly manage interfaces, project managers should attempt to do the following:

- Size up overall needs.
- Define static interfaces.
- Establish early control of design.
- Emphasize project flexibility.
- Adapt the organization.
- Manage design and production.
- Control dynamic interfaces.

A Simplified Life-Cycle View of Interfacing

Since interfaces can be either static and ongoing or dynamic and transient, emphasis on interfacing varies throughout the project's life cycle. Early in the project, concern centers on developing a game plan, building team spirit, and working to achieve objectives. During implementation, attention shifts to routine coordination, maintaining group spirit, and generally staying on course. At the end of the project, a major concern is to develop an objective demobilization program that is sensitive to all parties' needs. Table 7-1 shows a simplified breakdown of interfacing needs and situations for each major phase in the project's life cycle.

Monitoring Interfacing Needs

When projects veer off course, resulting in overruns and discontent, the causes can usually be traced to one of two

Table 7–1. Sample of interfacing needs and solutions related to major phases of the project's life cycle.

Phase	Interfacing Needs	Interfacing Solutions
"Start"	Establish game plan, team spirit, objectives.	Use participative macroplanning, consensus management, team-building techniques, kick-off seminars, intensive on-the-job coaching.
"Run"	Maintain routine coordination; keep up the spirit; stay on course. Dynamic interfacing.	Conduct periodic project review meetings, project audits, design reviews, frequent coordination meetings, ongoing training.
"Stop"	Establish objective demobilization plan; understand mutual needs.	Conduct demobilization and shutdown review meetings; interview client and affected parties; prepare shutdown checklists and formal close-out procedures.

sources. Either basic project functions aren't being performed adequately (for example, the designers are poor designers) or project interfacing efforts are inadequate (the boundaries of project activities aren't being crossed). In other words, trouble arises from either substandard performance of independent functions or inadequate coordination of those functions.

A "macromonitoring" effort is needed to spot problems before they become unmanageable. Standard control systems normally focus on details rather than on the sometimes-subjective information that also influences major management moves. To perceive the overall project in its true light, periodic overviews are necessary. This implies utilizing a nonroutine approach or special event to focus needed attention on potential problems. Samples of overview events designed to size up project status are given in the following text.

Design Reviews

Good engineering management practices can shed revealing light on areas of drooping project performance. Reviews of (1) technical feasibility, (2) value engineering, and (3) constructability of design are standard methods for pinpointing engineering interface problems. The prevailing question in *technical feasibility reviews* is: "Will it work?" The review covers design criteria and technical assumptions and includes spot checks of detailed drawings. *Value engineering reviews* are aimed at evaluating the cost effectiveness of design and include such exercises as comparing the cost advantages of specifying, say, structural steel versus reinforced concrete. *Constructability reviews* focus on the design/construction interface and question design criteria from the constructor's standpoint by asking, "How efficiently can it be built?" The purpose is to determine if, by making acceptable adjustments in design, construction time and cost can be reduced.

Situation Audits

A good way for upper management to get a handle on a project is through the project situation audit, also known as the performance audit. The project management audit is a thorough fact-finding exercise aimed at unearthing information and examining a project's progress. As in other audits, the object is to evaluate the status of ongoing operations. Such audits are done on an as-needed basis to identify problems that require review and adjustment at the strategic level.

While procedures may vary from project to project, these principles are generally applicable to large project audits:

1. The audit lasts from two to three days.
2. It is sponsored or carried out by senior-level personnel not directly involved in the project.
3. The objective is to pinpoint and correct major problem areas in order to reverse negative project trends.
4. Performance of each activity area is analyzed along with the corresponding interfaces.

The audit's objective is to reveal the project's true status. It is not to collect incriminating evidence to identify those "guilty" of failing to meet project goals. This goal, if appropriately communicated, helps break down defensive stances that some project team members might assume. The following list suggests some potentially fruitful targets for project audits:

♦ Detailed project plans
♦ Procedures for monitoring and control
♦ Contingency allowances and risk
♦ Project staffing
♦ Internal interfaces
♦ Reporting arrangements
♦ Client relations
♦ Subcontractor and vendor relations

 ♦ Third-party relations
 ♦ Accounting, invoicing, and billing[3]

Periodic Reviews

The periodic review is a variation of the performance audit that is carried out on a regularly scheduled basis. It may be carried out quarterly, semiannually, or at other intervals, and is conducted by a specially constituted board, council, or other high-level group. The management group attempts to meet the following objectives:

 ♦ To make the project manager formally accountable on a periodic basis.
 ♦ To give the project manager an opportunity to be heard by high-level executives directly or indirectly involved in the project.
 ♦ To allow upper managers to exchange ideas with company executives on project policies and major interfacing flaws.

The periodic review fills the need for high-level interfacing and helps the project team meet broad project goals.

Interfacing Through Expediting

Expediting is often associated with follow-up visits made at manufacturing plants for adding an extra push to ensure timely delivery by vendors. Expediting can play a critical role in successfully managing a wide variety of activities, including: engineering, procurement, and construction schedules; estimating and cost engineering; quality assurance and quality control; and claims management.

In this broader sense, expediting is designed to hurry along numerous project activities. Because boundaries are usually traversed in the process of gathering information and spurring others to action, expediting is in fact a detailed interfacing effort. Expediting results in the following benefits:

- Improved engineering interfaces
- Improved probability of attaining schedules
- Reduced costs from delays or disruptions
- Establishment of history file to minimize claims
- Establishment of vendor lead time records
- Assurance that test and inspection records are completed and retained[4]

Final Steps

Here are specific action items considered important for the project manager to ensure an integrated project effort:

1. Plan for integration.
2. Develop an integrated work breakdown structure, schedule, and budget.
3. Continually review and update the project plan.
4. Assure adherence to the project plan.
5. Resolve conflict situations.
6. Remove roadblocks.
7. Set priorities.
8. Make administrative and technical decisions across interfaces.
9. Solve customer or client problems.
10. Assure that project transfer takes place.
11. Maintain communication links across interfaces.[5]

These action items help orient interfacing efforts. Since interfacing is fundamentally artistic and not scientific, fixing hard-and-fast rules is a subjective exercise. Just as artists create through unique and mysterious processes, project managers integrate people and undertakings by using sometimes nebulous and oblique techniques. How that essential integration is attained is not of major importance. It can be done unconventionally or "by the book," but projects must be integrated for the prescribed goals to be met. Here are some general principles applicable for achieving that integration through project interfacing:

- Learn how client and/or upper management personnel feel about the project. What are their views? Their biases?
- Start the project with a macroscale participative planning approach.
- Develop a formal integration plan that includes project "blending" techniques such as integration workshops, training efforts, and coaching sessions.
- Pinpoint major areas requiring interfacing and assign responsibilities to individuals for monitoring those efforts.
- Schedule periodic project overviews, management audits, and routine coordination meetings.
- Make provisions for expediting efforts when activities get "bogged down."

Because no one individual has the authority required to interface all project activities, a team effort must be generated to span project boundaries.

References

1. Justo Calari, "Friend or Foe? The Contractor and the Consultant," *Worldwide Projects* (April–May 1978), p. 66.
2. The entire discussion of static and dynamic interfacing is adapted from Peter W. G. Morris, "Interface Management—An Organization Theory Approach to Project Management," *Project Management Quarterly,* vol. 10, no. 2 (June 1979), pp. 27–37.
3. M. Ruskin and W. Eugene Estes, "The Project Management Audit: Its Role and Conduct," *Project Management Institute Proceedings* (October 1982), p. V-G.2.

4. Robert C. Julian and Clyde D. Grim, Jr., "Expediting—A Tool for Mature Project Managers," *Project Management Institute Proceedings* (October 1982), p. V-F.1.

5. Linn C. Stuckenbruck, *The Implementation of Project Management: The Professional's Handbook* (Reading, Mass.: Addison-Wesley, 1981), p. 146.

Chapter 8

Using Managerial Time

Time is the most undefinable yet paradoxical of
things; the past is gone, the future has not come,
and the present becomes the past even while
we attempt to define it, and, like the flash of
the lightning, at once exists and expires.

Caleb C. Colton

There's Not Enough Time in the Day

The wail of the harried project manager echoes throughout
the office: "If the day only had thirty-six hours, I could
really get on top of things!" The project manager is probably
the most sought-after individual in the place. The PM is the
project hub; an endless list of subordinate activities converges
on that hub, including design, project engineering, supply,
implementation, planning and scheduling, and logistical and
support systems. The PM is also solicited by the client,
government regulatory agencies, special consultants, financing agencies, joint venture partners, local authorities, and
anyone else who wants to deal with the "person in charge."

Project managers and project team members tend to be
by nature highly effective, objective individuals with track
records that demonstrate achievement—otherwise they would

be working in other fields. But even the most effective project managers can optimize output by reviewing their time-management programs. In most cases a preliminary analysis reveals that, with a few adjustments, the manager can produce even more while expending considerably less effort. This form of optimization is often termed "working smarter."

This chapter establishes guidelines for managing the project team members' most fundamental resource—their own time. Time management is explored from the project manager's perspective and includes basic philosophies about time, evaluation of the manager's present time habits, suggestions for unplugging major bottlenecks, and recommendations for improving time-management approaches and practices.

Linear Time vs. Natural Time

The invention of time-measuring devices created the concept of *linear time* and what might be called in modern times "living by the clock." Linear time is contrary to natural time, which is instinctive and governed by the oscillations of nature and the biological and social milestones of life. Living on linear time is a learned discipline and is contrary to man's natural way of dealing with the periods marked by the turning of the globe.[1] With the advent of the Industrial Age, the need for more production at less cost sparked a desire to increase productivity, which can be measured by the number of units produced in a given period of time.

Modern-day project management is fundamentally an outgrowth of the more recent Industrial Age and reflects the industrialists' concern for getting a job done within a given time frame. Perhaps the only truly significant breakthrough in project time analytics came with the successful application of planning and scheduling networks in the space-age developments of the early 1960s. Project people were then able to identify and evaluate specific time requirements and cross-relate activities using a network. It then became possible to determine with a greater degree of accuracy "what should be done when."

In applying sophisticated network planning and scheduling systems, project team members, including the project manager, find themselves caught between the idea of linear time—a learned chronological concept—and natural time, which resonates with a deeper, unclocked perception of human life. This inner conflict, reflecting the inability of most people to fully program themselves on linear time, is one hypothesis for explaining why people are often incapable of making things happen within the dictates of the insensitive, "unnatural" linear time system.

The Insurmountable Task

How can key project people handle this challenge? How can they become fully attuned to the project's time needs? More importantly, how do they manage their own time? If systems exist for scheduling and controlling projects' linear time needs, do the PMs have similar systems for dealing with perhaps the most important of all project resources, their own managerial time? Are the principles of planning and scheduling that are accepted as basic tenets for managing projects applied with the same fervor by team members when they organize their own workdays?

Often, the PM may feel that the challenge is insurmountable. Given the constraints of time, quality, cost, and political environment, the PM faces a daily barrage of ambiguities and "impossible" tasks, all of which are supposed to be fielded routinely while calmly planning the next strategic project move. A 36-hour day would better fit the PM's driving schedule, rather than the sparse 24 hours that must also accommodate personal and family life.

The time crunch felt by the project manager may have logical explanations. After all, by circumstance and design, the PM is the center of project activities. The PM's hand (or nose) finds its way into countless areas varying from minor to major importance. As the chronometer ticks away, the day's hours seem to shrink, crises mount, and people and telephones clamor for a few moments of the PM's time. The PM's time-management habits have far-reaching effects. The pace for the project staff is set by the PM's style. The ability to set and meet goals and deadlines and to achieve high productivity are also directly influenced. Attitudes toward meetings, paper-handling, and interruptions are likewise triggered by the PM's time-management moves.

All of the classic time-management barriers of excess paperwork, overloaded meeting schedules, extensive one-on-one interviews, and constant interruptions must be hurdled by the PM. If a path can be cleared through some of those obstacles, more energies can be shifted from reacting (responding to actions initiated by others) to proacting (taking initiative on subjects which will ultimately result in project benefit). A weeding-out system is needed to separate nonproductive time consumers from those few important subjects that are truly worthy of attention. For the project manager, this is particularly difficult because of the great number of activities administered.

Yet for some, the task doesn't seem to be as difficult. A special knack, bordering on genius, seems to enable a few PMs to direct projects to timely and successful completion in spite of a climate of apparent managerial chaos. These PMs have inborn or developed abilities for making the right managerial moves—including mapping out strategic planning, motivating others, team building, delegating, and developing systems. Somehow time is available to tend to the important project issues and get the job done.

Most PMs are not blessed with "magical" abilities, and find that systematically eliminating major time bottlenecks and rearranging daily priorities can spark an increase in project output. The average PM endowed with reasonable professional talents can boost productivity considerably by heeding simple hints drawn from the literature on executive time management. The survey results given in this chapter imply an existing concern on the part of project management professionals regarding the need to improve time-management practices.

The Survey

A time-management survey was conducted at the Joint Project Management Institute/INTERNET Symposium held in Boston, in October 1981, where over 800 project management professionals from around the world attended three days of debates and discussions on project management.[2] Four hundred questionnaires were distributed during the event and 78 completed forms were returned. About a third of the respondents worked in manufacturing-related industries at the time of the survey. The remaining respondents were evenly distributed among architects and engineers (A&Es), contractors, independent consultants, and miscellaneous other categories.

Of the 78 respondents, 31 were professionals carrying the title of project director or project manager. The remaining fell into the following categories: president or member of the board, vice president or manager, chief engineer or construction manager, department or section head in a project structure, functional department or section head, consultant, or professor. Thirty-eight respondents indicated they had between 10 and 20 years of experience in project management. Seventeen of those surveyed had more than 30 years of experience. The remainder had worked for less than 10 years in project management.

Time Usage

The group put in an average workday of slightly more than nine hours. Meetings were the major time consumer, taking up slightly less than two hours daily. Routine paperwork, telephone conversations, closed-door concentration, and one-on-one interactions each took up between 65 and 81 minutes per day and represented major time consumers for the respondents. The remaining one quarter of the respondents' workday was distributed evenly among items of lesser impact, as shown in Table 8-1.

Table 8-1. Time distribution of respondents' average workday.

Activity	Minutes per Day Spent on Activity	Percentage of Time Spent on Activity
Routine paperwork	81	15%
Telephone conversations	65	12
Meetings	108	20
Closed-door concentration for planning, analysis, and control	65	12
One-on-one discussions, interviews, or coaching sessions	75	14
Coffee, chats, rest stops	22	4
Business lunches extending over normal lunch periods	11	2
Time-consuming conversations and interruptions	32	6
Travel (time spent en route during working hours)	16	3
Reading professional literature	22	4
Unaccounted for	27	5
Other	16	3
TOTAL	540	100%

Personal Philosophy

The respondents were asked to assign "points" to items 1, 2, and 3 below to indicate the relative contribution each item makes to their own personal time philosophy.

Personal Time Philosophy	Percentage of Total Philosophy
"I determine how I use my time."	46.4%
"Others determine how I use my time."	25.9
"The system determines how I use my time."	27.7
	100.0%

The results indicate that more than half of the respondents' composite time philosophy is made up of views that accept that time is outside their personal control (items 2 and 3, which together equal 53.6 percent). On the other hand, the remaining component of 46.4 percent reflects a strong independent factor in the respondents' philosophies.

When asked to identify the items that represented the most serious causes of time-management problems, respondents indicated the following, listed in order of importance:

1. Difficulty of saying *no*
2. Lack of self-discipline
3. Lack of time-management awareness in the organization
4. Less than fully competent employees
5. Excessive bureaucracy in the organization
6. Poor utilization of secretary or assistant
7. Tendency to centralize, rather than delegate

Search for Solutions

The respondents were given five solutions to the problem of dealing with an increased work load and asked to arrange them in order of effectiveness, starting with the one they considered best. The results are as follows:

1. Delegate more (involve others).
2. Do less work (eliminate some work items).
3. Let things slide (delay).
4. Work longer (more hours).
5. Work harder (faster).

Scheduling Daily Activities

When asked to indicate which phrase best reflected their thoughts on scheduling daily activities, the respondents replied as follows:

"I schedule all activities daily and allot specific periods of time for each [*14 percent of the respondents*]."
"I list 'to-do' items but don't allocate specific time periods [*51 percent of the respondents*]."

"I carry my agenda in my head [3 *percent of the re-*
spondents]."
"I note some items on the agenda, but most of the day
is not formally scheduled [*32 percent of the respon-*
dents]."

Thus, the majority of the professionals polled (51 percent) indicated they did not formally schedule daily activities, although they did prepare lists of things to do. Only
14 percent responded that their workday was fully scheduled. Almost one-third showed partial scheduling practices
and only 3 percent avoided any effort to schedule daily
activities on paper.

Project Priorities

The following hypothetical problem was presented to
those surveyed:

As project manager for a $100 million industrial plant
which is four months behind schedule, assuming you had
made the following to-do list on a given day, give the
sequence in which you would perform the work items (number from one to twelve).

The following order represents a composite of the individual responses:

1. Analyze progress report to determine appropriate
   corrective measures.
2. Think about how to get back on schedule.
3. Review milestone dates.
4. Approve drawings for release to contractor.
5. Listen to contractor's complaints on interference.
6. Sign checks for paying suppliers.
7. Review project management organization to see how
   it can better meet the needs.
8. Read and sign correspondence.
9. Lobby with the client.
10. Draft reply to nasty letter from client.
11. Interview junior engineers.

12. Read revision 4 to the construction manual.

Delegation

The two most important reasons for delegating, according to the survey's respondents, are:

- To increase managerial effectiveness
- To provide stimulus to subordinates

Other items that were considered important, but to a lesser degree, were:

- To allow time to think
- To expand my horizons
- To avoid a "one-man-band" tendency

Justifications given by the respondents for not delegating to a greater extent were:

- Subjects are too confidential to involve others.
- My subordinates aren't sufficiently qualified.
- I can do it better.
- I already delegate enough.

Meetings

The survey showed that the participants attended over six meetings per week. In those meetings an average of 25 percent of the time was spent engaging in off-the-track banter, generalized complaining, lobbying for pet causes, and other unproductive activities.

When the respondents were asked, "What do you think contributed to the eventual nonproductiveness of the last meeting you attended?" the three most prevalent responses were:

- Improperly planned meeting (no written objective or detailed agenda)

- ♦ Inept leadership
- ♦ Undisciplined participants

Solutions

Respondents listed the following items in order of importance as ways to solve time-related problems or improve the use of managerial time.

1. Question whether certain things should be done at all.
2. Start being more disciplined in avoiding interruptions.
3. Start using an agenda regularly.
4. Delegate more.
5. Eliminate as much paperwork as possible.
6. Start closing the door to the office.

The sequence selected suggests a general awareness that there's not enough time to do it all. Yet the reluctance to close the office door indicates a tendency to engage in hands-on management. If priorities are indeed as reflected above, the poll mirrors the managers' expectations that the use of time *can* be optimized without creating excessive communication barriers.

Cornerstones of Time Management

Dozens of books on executive time management are available to tell business professionals how to manage their workday (or, more correctly perhaps, how to manage *themselves* during the day). Some works extend the concepts to life management, laying out guidelines for a more personal approach to handling time. Others present specific how-to procedures and map out the route to successful use of time for a special audience, such as business executives, hospital administrators, or working mothers. Although aimed at differing audiences, the books carry common themes that are held by many authors to be universally applicable. Selected major topics from the literature are summarized in the following discussion.

How Is Time Used?

Peter F. Drucker suggests in the training film *Management Time* that managers make a time log and register for a week how each day's time is spent.[3] He recommends that a secretary or assistant jot down the boss's time usage, or that the manager make notes throughout the day. A review of the time log at week's end generally reveals that time is misused, as the following usually has occurred:

- Snap judgments are made on highly important subjects.
- Telephone conversations go on and on.
- There are periods of incessant interruptions during which virtually nothing of significance is accomplished.
- There is a tendency to dwell on unimportant subjects that could well be delegated or ignored.
- There are periods of paper slavery in which much unnecessary paper is handled.

In the film, Drucker indicates that when the manager is confronted with the facts of how time is *really* spent during the week, he or she is forced to reflect and improve time habits. The time log serves as an "awareness bell" for awakening the manager and making him take stock of actual time-management habits. The log is simply a prop—though highly effective according to Drucker—to motivate managers to tackle bottlenecks and formulate a truly proactive management stance.

Time Barriers

Four major time barriers are found to dominate many managers' days:

- ◆ Correspondence that must be read and/or signed
- ◆ Meetings, scheduled or otherwise
- ◆ One-on-one listening, problem solving, or coaching
- ◆ Telephone calls, incoming and outgoing

Gaining time means aiming a steely eye at each bottleneck in an effort to sweep away wasted motions and time killers. Some pointers for keeping precious minutes from the major time consumers are given as follows:

1. *Ask yourself if you really need to see all that paper.* Just because it lands on your desk doesn't mean you should spend time with it. With your secretary's aid, make a list of all documents that cross your desk and classify the subjects in groups of priorities A, B, and C. Then, by delegating, eliminating, and condensing, drastically reduce the time spent on C items and, to a lesser degree, on those of group B, thus freeing up time for A priorities.

2. *Discipline your meetings for more effective results in less time.* Go back to the basics. Does everybody know what the subject and objective of the meeting are? It's amazing how many people don't know what the meeting is all about (sometimes not even the leader has a clear idea). See that project group leaders know the fundamentals of running a meeting. Establish meeting objectives clearly in a memo, meeting notice, or other written form. Prior to the meeting make an itemized agenda and afterward register the results with meeting notes. Avoid "instantaneous problem solving." Direct the discussion initially toward alternate solutions in order to explore the full potential. Create an open atmosphere in which all ideas are valid. Once this stage of exploration is completed, have the group focus in on one solution. The result may be a better solution obtained by consensus. Time is ultimately saved because the procedure tends to minimize entrenched argumentations and stand-off positions.

3. *Determine how much time you have for one-on-one listening, problem solving, and coaching; then ration your time accordingly.* Do you have to receive all those who wander into your office for as long as they wish? Obviously

not. Many of your visitors should be talking to one of your subordinates. You have a perfect prerogative to establish time limits for your interviews. Your secretary can help articulate your interview agenda. This approach should not eliminate periods when an open-door policy, essential for project pulse-taking, exists.

4. *Establish a telephone code of conduct.* Steer clear of being a slave to the telephone. Group your outgoing calls to get them out of the way. Avoid incoming call interruptions when you're working on important matters (call back at a specified time). If you have to make daily long-distance calls, try scheduling them for a specific hour of the day. Avoid grabbing the phone on impulse—organize your thoughts and discuss all subjects with a given party in an orderly sequence.

The pointers given suggest that a manager's workday can be optimized simply by limiting time used in paperwork, meetings, one-on-one contacts, and telephone conversations. These suggestions capture many of the classic time-management solutions that are also applicable in the project management world. Management experts contend that by applying the principles exemplified in the suggestions given, more time will be available for working on important project matters.

Such a "formula" approach may be regarded as simplistic, however. Due to the wide diversity in PMs' styles, personalities, backgrounds, prior successes and failures, and aspirations, a ready-made time-management posture cannot fit all situations. Rather, a tailor-made approach is needed, with the PM acting as designer, selecting those pointers that are consistent with his or her own projected managerial profile.

The Time Matrix

Project managers need to be able to separate the wheat from the chaff. Adequate time must be spent on the "wheat," that is, the subjects most relevant to the goals of the project. Often, however, these subjects are pushed aside in order to make room for mini-urgencies, the "chaff." Such urgencies are characterized by a pressing need for given activities to be completed within a short time span—regardless of whether the activities are trivial or important. An abundance of urgent items over an extended period generally carries the indelible stamp of sloppy planning and poor management.

The question arises, however, on the relationship between importance and urgency. Isn't an urgent subject automatically important and an important one therefore urgent? Figure 8-1 is an importance/urgency matrix that helps put the connection between the two concepts into perspective. The matrix shows four distinct relationships between urgency and importance. *Quadrant 1* indicates a crisis situation in which a subject is both important and urgent—for example, a major casting flaw in a critical-path equipment item or a client who wants to make a major design change. *Quadrant 2* represents the planning and control mode—the subjects, while important, aren't red-flagged with urgency. Concerns about areas such as basic planning, training sessions, and development of subordinates would be part of this quadrant. *Quadrant 3* encompasses subjects that are relatively unimportant but carry the urgent label. Many telephone calls, one-on-one conversations, and pieces of correspondence labeled "urgent" fall into this category. *Quadrant 4* represents genuine time-wasters—items that are unimportant and not urgent. Examples of these subjects are overemphasis on procedures, excessive efficiency, and extended chats about a football game.

A typical time distribution shows problems in quadrant 1 demanding and receiving their fair share of attention, while those in quadrant 2 are siphoned off by the trivia and time-wasters of quadrants 3 and 4. The result is insufficient planning and control, and subsequently there are more crises and urgent trivia. The logical solution for breaking out of this circle is to concentrate on the important matters found in quadrants 1 and 2. This action will help attenuate the negative effects of the time-gobbling problems in quadrants 3 and 4.

Figure 8-1. Importance/urgency matrix.

	Important	Not Important
Urgent	1	3
Not Urgent	2	4

Source: Merrill E. Douglass and Donna N. Douglass, *Manage Your Time, Manage Your Work, Manage Yourself* (New York: AMACOM, 1980), p. 74.

Pareto's Principle

Pareto's principle has applications in numerous fields, including sales, materials management, and maintenance. Simply stated, Pareto's principle is that the significant items in a given group normally represent a relatively small percentage of the total items in the group.

Pareto's principle establishes criteria for discrimination when one is confronted with a large number of items. With the items arranged in groups of *A*, *B*, and *C*, where group *A* represents the most important subjects. Pareto's principle applied to managerial time yields the distribution in Figure 8-2. This 70-20-10 percentage is a commonly used rule of thumb for distributions according to Pareto's principle. Pareto's principle applied to time management indicates that *unequal* treatment should be given to the various subjects confronting the PM. According to the standard distribution outlined in Pareto's principle, up to 70 percent of the PM's time should be applied to group A subjects. In project work, sample group A topics are:

♦ Selecting key staff members
♦ Developing project plans

Figure 8-2. Pareto's principle as applied to time allocation by project managers.

Subject Groups	Percentage of Subjects That Fall into Group	Percentage of Time That Should be Allocated to Group
A	10	70
B	20	20
C	70	10

- Establishing overall project relationships
- Reviewing project budget requirements
- Making decisions regarding project control systems
- Establishing reporting criteria
- Developing and motivating staff

Subjects in groups B and C represent lower priority topics that might be delegated or abbreviated. These subjects should be put into their proper perspective with corresponding allocation of only 20 percent and 10 percent of management time, respectively.

Scheduling Time vs. Work

After a day of little or no forward progress, many PMs have asked themselves, "What did I really accomplish today?" The answer is often not encouraging. One explanation is that the PM is led astray by the whims and urgencies of others, thus draining time from more pertinent subjects. Drucker takes the position that managers don't accomplish what they should because their approach is wrong: They try to cram an ever-expanding mass (all the work that comes at them from sundry directions) into a limited, unstretchable compartment (their productive workday). Drucker contends that *the work* should be trimmed and prioritized.[4] Trying to make time expand is somewhat like trying to pour more water into a glass than it will hold. It's no wonder that no matter how hard some PMs drive, they still find themselves up to their earlobes in work and complain that 24 hours a day are not enough!

Therefore plan your time first, then the work. In other words, you should lay out the day in terms of specific blocks of time, then fit priority items (relevant important subjects) into those time periods. For the less important subjects, figure out another way to get them done (delegate, reorganize, eliminate, and so on).

Conclusion

Project managers occupy extremely demanding positions. The PM's time is sought by almost everyone involved in the project; therefore, it must be managed effectively. There are no magic formulas for improving management productivity, but the principles for bettering time usage are elementary; PMs who are capable of dominating complicated and esoteric project concepts can easily put time-management rules into effect.

The survey results given show the respondents' awareness of the need to effectively manage time. Ideas for improving time habits can be grouped into the following major points:

- ◆ Learn how time is really being used (make a time log).
- ◆ Limit time consumers such as correspondence, meetings, one-on-one contacts, and phone calls.
- ◆ Use time on a prioritized, scheduled basis, giving emphasis to important items over those that appear urgent.

John Quincy Adams said in *The Hour Glass,* "Time was—
Time shall be—drain the glass—but where in Time is now?"[5]
The project manager's time dilemma is captured in Adams'
concept of fleeting "nowness." For project requirements to
be met, the PM's time perception must be keen and time-
management habits solid. Attention to the PM's own time
habits can spark a productivity payoff, leading the way to
quality projects completed within budget and on schedule.

References

1. Sebastian de Grazia, *Of Time, Work, & Leisure* (New
   York: The Twentieth Century Fund, 1962), pp.
   318–325.
2. Paul C. Dinsmore, "The Project Manager's Time
   Quandary: Survey Results and Suggested Solutions,"
   Project Management Institute Proceedings (Toronto,
   1982), pp. IV-J.1-9.
3. Peter F. Drucker, in the training film *Management
   Time* (Rockville, Md.: BNA Communications Inc.,
   1968).
4. Peter F. Drucker, *O Gerente Eficaz* (Rio de Janeiro,
   Brazil: Zahar Editores, 1978), pp. 33–61.
5. Henry Davidoff, *The Pocket Book of Quotations* (New
   York: Pocket Books, 1952), p. 399.

Chapter 9

Handling Conflict

Conflict, like power, is one of those fascinating but frequently abused and misunderstood subjects. Like any potent force, conflict generates ambivalence by virtue of its ability to do great injury or, if harnessed, great good.

Kenneth Thomas

Conflict and People

Conflict is an offspring of disagreement between individuals. It is basic to human behavior—inevitable in all endeavors involving people. Each unique person is bound to have views that differ from those of others. And differing views tend to generate conflict, which may range from mild irritation to no-holds-barred defiance.

Conflict requires that something be at stake. If an opposing party's action reduces the other party's chances of winning the stakes, then conflict increases. If the outcome is important and the actions of each party block the other from fulfilling its hopes, then both parties feel the value of the outcome is reduced, and the potential for conflict is increased.

Traditional and Contemporary Views of Conflict

Views of conflict can be divided into opposing schools called *traditional* and *contemporary*. In the traditional view, friction is seen as a negative situation caused by trouble-makers. Whenever possible, efforts must be made to avoid or suppress conflict. In the contemporary view, conflict is inevitable, and if properly handled can actually foster positive results. Conflict is a natural product of change and should be accepted as such.

In project management, the contemporary view tends to prevail; yet even within this line of thought, conflict can be seen both positively and negatively. Conflict is positive when it helps to resolve a problem or lends support to efforts to meet goals. Conflict is detrimental, however, when resources or energies are applied and the corresponding outcome yields little or no forward progress.

Types of Conflicts

Project conflicts can be grouped into three major categories: (1) intrapersonal, where the individual struggles internally with conflict that may or may not be caused or affected by others, (2) interpersonal, where interaction takes place between individuals, and (3) intergroup, where departments or other groups are at odds. A brief description of these common project conflict modes follows.

♦ *Intrapersonal conflict.* Conflict occurs within an individual when personal, professional, or job-related expectations or hopes are frustrated. The conflict may stem from personal limitations or anxieties that have nothing to do with the project. If inner conflicts do not overflow and turn into interpersonal clashes, they may remain latent and actually not affect the project at all.

♦ *Interpersonal conflict.* This may originate from differences in project management styles, competing aspirations, or personality differences. Interpersonal conflicts involve two or more people and can focus on just about anything. This type of friction calls for custom made solutions, which depend on the specific situations and the players.

♦ *Intergroup conflict.* When one group or team is pitted against another, intergroup conflict results. Just about any subject, whether or not it's related to the project, can be the cause of the conflict. Intergroup conflicts are normally the result of interpersonal friction between influential project leaders. They can be partially managed by dealing with the conflict on a personal basis through those influential leaders.

While conflict may be *exclusive,* with only one type existing at a given time, two or more types might also occur simultaneously. For instance, an intrapersonal conflict over a project cost/quality trade-off ("Should I take the risk?") could set off an interpersonal clash. This might consequently cause respective staff groups to rally around the major participants, touching off an intergroup dispute.

Conflicts in Project Management

Although conflict crops up in all human endeavors, projects may offer environments particularly susceptible to generating strife. What are the reasons for conflicts in project work? Thamhain and Wilemon conducted extensive research on conflict in project management. In an article published in *Sloan Management Review,* they identify the following seven primary focal points for project conflict.[1]

1. *Project priorities.* Differing views over activity sequence for accomplishing project goals
2. *Administrative procedures.* Differences regarding how the project will be managed, including reporting and interface relationships, definition of responsibilities, and procedures for administrative support
3. *Technical opinions and performance trade-offs.* Disagreements over technical issues, performance specifications, technical trade-offs, and performance issues

4. *Manpower resources.* Differing viewpoints on staffing and personnel utilization
5. *Cost objectives.* Disagreements over cost estimates from support areas
6. *Schedules.* Disagreements related to timing, sequencing, and scheduling of project-related tasks
7. *Personality.* Interpersonal differences as opposed to technical issues; often ego-centered

The Dynamic Characteristic of Project Conflict

In different phases of the project's life cycle there are different sources of conflict. Early in the project, priorities are the reason for differing opinions. As work progresses, the project's schedule begins to draw attention. Manpower allocation also becomes an increasing source of conflict as the project progresses.

On a project-wide basis, however, research findings by Thamhain and Wilemon show that disagreements over schedules offered the most persistent conflicts, followed by project priorities and manpower. Technical, support, and cost topics fill the middle of the list, which is rounded out by personality conflicts in last place.[2]

Except for personality conflicts, all other sources cited in the findings constitute the technical and administrative bases for managing projects. All are related to achieving the project's objectives of quality, time, and cost. The survey results thus show the project's objectives themselves to be the root of most conflicts.

"Soft" Causes for Conflict

While conflict can be correlated with measurable sources such as schedule, cost, and manpower, there are also "softer," less tangible reasons for discord. Human comportment and behavioral characteristics can be the cause for dissidence.

"Hard" and "soft" views, although different, are closely intertwined. The "hard" view focuses on the palpable issues of project conflict and answers the question, "What topics

are the focus of conflicts?" The soft approach aims at identifying more subjective criteria, nestled in the subtleties of
human nature, in the hopes of answering the query, "What
is the behavioral causation of the conflict?"

To affirm that the true causes of project conflict are the
"hard" objective factors or, alternatively, that "soft" reasons
are the real causes of project disharmony is to set off an
argument similar to the "chicken and the egg" enigma. It
is inconsequential whether the soft causes or the hard causes
come first, but it is important to distinguish between the
two types and size up conflict causes not only from the
"hard" viewpoint, but also from the less tangible behavioral
outlook. Paul A. Orleman gives additional causes for conflict
that lean toward the softer views, summarized as follows:

- Lack of clear understanding of project objectives, both
  global and specific, for the work breakdown packages
- Diversity of disciplinary expertise on a project team
- Ambiguity over specific roles among the support departments
- Power of reward and punishment possessed by the
  project manager
- The project's threat to the traditional mission of a
  functional area
- Lack of perceived relationships between the project's
  goals and top management's goals
- Lack of open support for the project by senior management
- Delegating a technical decision upward, which makes
  it likely to receive a political solution[3]

From a "people-side" analysis, human behavior is at the
root of all project discord and tends to set off the hard causes
of conflict.

Effects of Conflict

Conflict has a beneficial effect when it results in directly
furthering a project's progress or indirectly serving as a

catalyst for achieving a project's objectives. It is detrimental when it causes the project to lose momentum or creates situations that result in wasted efforts.

Benefits of Conflict

The positive value of conflict is underestimated. Properly managed, conflict is a valuable tool, particularly when conflictive situations are confronted in their early stages. At this point, emotional involvement is still low, and problems can be put to rest by straightforward rational approaches. If those same problems are allowed to fester, they may evolve into major project clashes.

Conflict in projects might be compared with pain in the human body. While pain is not usually praised as a boon to mankind, without it the human mortality rate would be sharply aggravated, since people would lack a built-in signaling device to advise of bodily malfunctions. Just as pain is relieved by proper corrective action, conflict—if dealt with promptly and effectively—will likewise be reduced or go away. If not, as in the case of bodily pain, it may grow worse, perhaps requiring major surgery and involving lengthy immobilization.

Aside from its role as a sensor, conflict has other positive effects. It offers increased challenge for finding new solutions and gives groups and individuals opportunities for jointly solving a project's problems. As groups rally around a cause, this stimulus can lead to uncovering new facts and information that can benefit the project. Conflict also acts as a "power monitor," allowing dissenting parties to size up relative strengths for use in future interactions.[4]

Dissent in projects, if handled properly, can constitute a fundamental tool for achieving results. In many cases, this simply involves managing conflict routinely and promptly as it appears. In other cases, however, the *instigation* of conflict might actually be called for. For instance, if key project planners are systematically putting off establishing basic milestone dates because they lack data, a push by the project manager to fix "best guess" dates may generate helpful feedback from other participating parties. Thrusting the subject into an arena of potential conflict may set off discussion that will ultimately lead to the timely establishment of those dates. In this case, conflict is purposely triggered to boost along a mired-down project activity.

Conflict usually starts as a murmur, but it may develop into a screeching yell. Conflict serves as a signal that something is wrong, thus calling for remedial action. This action may range from dramatically steering a yawing project back on course, to routinely dealing with the behavioral traits that cause strife in the project. The purpose of managing project conflict, therefore, is not to stamp it out, but to deal with it intelligently. Since reasonable levels of dissension are characteristic of healthy projects, team members must be attuned to handling it. In this way, the conflictive situations can ultimately be turned into benefits.

Detrimental Effects of Conflict

Conflict's negative repercussions may be easier to relate to than its benefits, since troubles and friction are generally considered to be synonymous with conflict. This unfavorable reputation is not without justification, of course, since conflict's adverse side, if not properly managed, can easily overpower potential blessings. Here are some of the drawbacks:

♦ *Conflict causes stress.* While part of thriving life forms, stress, in some cases, metes out an unhealthy aftermath. Stress affects humans both physically and emotionally, breeding ulcers, back pains, and other spurious palpitations. It brings on sleepless nights, irritable outbursts, and periods of inner withdrawal, taking its toll in bodily and mental strain.

♦ *Conflict creates an unproductive atmosphere.* In highly conflictive situations, people's productivity levels may fall because of the uncertainty generated by clashing views. As long as the conflict persists, confusion and ambiguity keep people from producing at their optimum.

♦ *Conflict may cause loss of status or position power.* Depending on how the conflict is handled and who the players are, disputes may put one of the parties in a "losing" pose. Paradoxically, this may mean a loss not only for the loser, but ultimately for the winner as well, because the winner has ongoing stakes in the project's overall success.

♦ *Conflicts tend to distort behavior among people.* In conflictive situations, people's sense of values may be substituted by an overzealous urge to find the facts. Prioritized management practices may be twisted into random decision making. Decisions may be enforced in an authoritarian environment. Loyalty may become more important than making the right managerial moves.

How to Resolve Conflicts in Project Management

There is no right way to settle conflicts. Conflict-resolving techniques range from the power-based "steamroller" approach to the more defensive tactical retreat. Intermediate views involve variations of side-stepping, give-and-take negotiating, and objective problem solving. Some modes are more fitting than others in given situations.

Blake and Mouton's general conflict-resolution techniques, presented in *The Managerial Grid®*, have been widely cited in project management literature. Those five ways of settling conflict—by withdrawing, smoothing, compromising, confronting, and forcing—offer an analytical base for sizing up specific project situations.[5] Interpretations of these conflict-resolution modes are given as follows:

♦ *Withdrawing* amounts to pulling out, retreating, or giving up. It may be used as a short-term tactic, to gain time, or as a strategic approach over longer time periods. Withdrawal is a passive, stop-gap way of dealing with conflict; it generally fails to solve the problem.

♦ *Smoothing* might be called the "tut-tut" or appeasing approach. It includes searching for common grounds of agreement while avoiding points of disagreement. Smoothing is aimed at keeping peace and avoiding outwardly conflictive situations. Since smoothing is only provisional in nature, it fails to provide a long-lasting solution to the underlying conflict.

♦ *Compromising* is bargaining. The objective is to reach an acceptable agreement. Even though that agreement may fall short of the ideal solution for each party, it presumably represents the best attainable understanding. Trade-off negotiation is commonly used in compromising. This means bargaining characterized by a philosophy of "I'll give you this if you'll give me that." When a compromise is reached and has been accepted as a just solution by the parties, then this technique can be said to have provided definitive resolution for conflict situations.

♦ *Confronting* is the problem-solving approach for resolving conflicts. Here the overriding philosophy is to pinpoint the problem and to objectively resolve it. Confrontation requires open dialog between participants, who must be both technically and managerially competent. Confrontation provides final solutions for conflict situations; it ultimately resolves the underlying problem.

♦ *Forcing* means using power to resolve conflict. The upshot of this approach is a win-lose situation in which one party clearly overwhelms the other. Forcing usually takes less time than, say, confrontation or compromising, yet it has the undesirable side effect of leaving hard feelings. Thus the conflict resolved by force may then come back to haunt the forcer at a later date. In spite of this drawback, forcing is another way of definitively resolving many conflicts.

In project management, which of the five conflict-resolution approaches should be favored and which should be avoided? Obviously, the one that works is the right conflict-management technique. The approach that removes barriers and clears the path for moving the project onward is the most adequate. Choosing the right alternative, however, is not easy, as the variables are many. Each situation is unique.

Personal characteristics, internal politics, individual goals and agenda, and existing relationships are factors that influence the manner in which conflicts are handled, thus making it difficult to set down hard-and-fast rules.

The Best Conflict-Solving Approach

The best apparent solution for settling project conflicts is the problem-solving or confrontation mode. Since project management consists fundamentally of resolving problems as the project evolves through its life cycle, this form of conflict settlement is ideal. The problem-solving view assumes that a "win-win" situation is always best because both the project and the parties involved come out ahead.

Quick agreement generally results when both parties have a problem-solving, or confrontation, attitude. Agreement also occurs when both parties share a compromising frame of mind. Stalemates predominate, however, when both parties have a forcing, smoothing, or withdrawal attitude. Confrontation is shown to be a strong resolution technique to use against other conflict-handling modes, with the exception of forcing, which may tend to overpower the confrontation mode. Forcing is a strong technique except when used against another forcing party, in which a stalemate tends to prevail. The compromiser yields to the problem-solver or forcer, but comes to agreement with the compromiser, smoother, or withdrawer. Smoothing, on the other hand, prevails over withdrawing, yet yields to confrontation, forcing, and compromising. Withdrawal yields to all other forms of conflict resolution, with the exception of withdrawal itself, in which case a stalemate results.[6]

Thomas-Kilmann Conflict Model

A model developed by Thomas and Kilmann classifies conflict-resolution modes in terms of concern for others' views versus concern for one's own views.[7] The terms applied to conflict-resolution modes in the Thomas-Kilmann model vary slightly from those used by Blake and Mouton; they correspond to one another as follows:

Avoidance, or withdrawal, corresponds to both a low concern for others' views and a low concern for one's own views. Accommodation, or smoothing, indicates a high concern for others' views and a lesser concern for one's own views. Compromising is characterized by a medium level of concern for both one's own and others' views. High concern for one's own views and for others' views corresponds to a collaborative or confrontation mode. A competitive or forcing style corresponds to a high concern for one's own views and a lesser concern for others'.

According to the Thomas-Kilmann model, each conflict-resolution strategy is appropriate for specific types of situations:

- Use avoidance (withdrawal):
  When you can't win.
  When the stakes are low.
  When the stakes are high, but you are not ready yet.
  To gain time.
  To unnerve your opponent.
  To preserve neutrality or reputation.
  When you think the problem will go away.
  When you win by delay.
- Use accommodation (smoothing):
  To reach an overarching goal.
  To create obligation for a trade-off at a later date.
  When the stakes are low.
  When liability is limited.
  To maintain harmony.
  When any solution will be adequate.
  To create goodwill (be magnanimous).
  When you'll lose anyway.
  To gain time.
- Use compromise:
  When both parties need to be winners.
  When you can't win.
  When others are as strong as you are.

When you haven't time to win.
To maintain your relationship with your opponent.
When you're not sure you are right.
When you get nothing if you don't.
When stakes are moderate.
To avoid giving the impression of "fighting."

♦ Use collaboration (confrontation):
When you both get at least what you wanted and
   maybe more.
To reduce costs.
To create a common power base.
To attack a common foe.
When skills are complementary.
When there is enough time.
When you want to preclude later use of other methods.
When there is trust.
When you have confidence in the other person's
   ability.
To maintain future relationships.

♦ Use a competitive approach (forcing):
When you are right.
When a "do or die" situation exists.
When stakes are high.
When important principles are at stake.
When you are stronger. (Never start a battle you can't
   win.)
To gain status or demonstrate power.
In short-term, one-shot deals.
When the relationship is unimportant.
When it's understood that a "game" is being played.[8]

Proactive Conflict Management

A proactive stance, however, is also needed to keep conflict
under control. This requires acting before conflict appears,
to minimize impact. Here are ideas for proactively managing
conflicts with some of the main project management players.

Minimizing Conflict With Subordinates

♦ *Discover your subordinates' personal and professional goals.* Whenever possible, associate workers' tasks with their own goals. For instance, microcomputer buffs could be given opportunities to use their interests on the job.

♦ *Make your expectations clear to your subordinates.* Clarify what you want and why you want it. Discuss criteria and ensure your message has been understood.

♦ *Define control parameters.* Discuss form, frequency, and intensity of control with your subordinates. Exercise control based on facts, not opinions.

♦ *Use mistakes as opportunities for training.* When errors occur, talk with the subordinate and ask for ideas and suggestions as to how such errors can be avoided in the future.

♦ *Give positive feedback.* Let your subordinates know you recognize their positive side. Avoid criticism. When you need to point out a weakness, make sure you balance your comments with positive input.

Minimizing Conflict With Your Colleagues

♦ *Help your colleagues meet their personal and professional goals.* Look for areas where interests are not conflictive; be supportive towards their objectives.

♦ *Establish a cooperative atmosphere.* Do favors for others, without concern for immediate return. When you do require support, they will be more likely to collaborate.

♦ *When you need help, give advance notice.* Justify your request in terms of company or project objectives; be accommodating to your colleagues' requirements.

♦ *Cultivate informal communications channels.* Have lunch together, develop non-work-related encounters, discuss topics other than daily work fare.

Minimizing Conflict With Clients And Users

♦ *Be supportive towards client representatives.* Your client or user may need data or information which you can readily supply. Be helpful, since you will surely need a sympathetic ear at some point during the project.

- *Maintain close contact with the client.* Avoid periods without communication. Clients require attention; when they don't get it, they tend to become more demanding.
- *Avoid surprises.* Unless you have good news, don't spring surprises. Let your clients know about problems and what you are doing to solve them. Deal with problems as they arise; don't let them build up.
- *Keep in touch at various levels.* Put directors in touch with directors, managers with managers, engineers with engineers, etc., and coordinate contacts between those levels.
- *Establish informal relationships with key client personnel.* Use encounters at lunches, dinners, social and sporting occasions to improve relationships with clients.
- *Conduct regular project status meetings.* Remember to include forecasts on future problems and needs. Meetings should be both informative and problem-solving in nature.

Minimizing Conflict With the Boss

- *Place yourself in the boss's spot.* What are the challenges and problems? Understand and be sympathetic to the pressures of upper management.
- *Analyze the boss's thinking patterns.* Does he or she think analytically or intuitively? To improve communications, remember to use approaches consistent with the boss's way of seeing things.
- *Don't take problems to the boss, take solutions.* Try to make his or her job easier. Analyze the situation, look at the alternative solutions, and make practical recommendations.
- *Keep the boss informed, both about what you've done and what you plan to do.* Even if you have full delegation of authority, your boss needs to know what is going on in your area.

- *Listen and observe.* Listen between the lines and watch body and facial language; look for the boss's real message.
- *Consult the boss on policy and criteria.* Ask for orientation, advice, and suggestions on matters of policy and management philosophy which may affect your work.
- *Don't steamroll the boss.* Use trial balloons; provide time for thinking and adjusting to your propositions. Provide data, be patient, and remember that timing can make or break a proposal.

Setting Off Conflict

All these suggestions, when applied to subordinates, colleagues, clients, and bosses, will help minimize the impact of negative conflict. They are proactive ideas, requiring "up front" initiative aimed at avoiding costly "patching up" operations later in the project cycle.

In some cases, however, a proactive stance may mean setting off conflict. Here are some examples when causing conflict is justifiable:

- *When there is no other apparent solution to the problem.* If the situation requires confrontation to be solved, then triggering conflict becomes a means to an end.
- *When the conflict will tend to grow if not tackled immediately.* Causing conflict while still manageable (as opposed to letting it take its course), keeps troubles from swelling out of proportion.
- *When apparent harmony covers up indecision and procrastination.* In this situation, if other approaches don't work, setting off conflict may be the way to get things moving.
- *When conflict can be used as a stimulus towards meeting goals.* Transforming conflict into healthy competition between groups, for instance, is a valid reason for stimulating conflict.

♦ When *conflict promises to contribute toward meeting project goals,* such as client satisfaction and quality, cost, and time targets. If conflict contributes towards attaining these objectives, then it should be triggered and subsequently managed.

Proactive management places project professionals in control of conflictive situations. Proaction means sitting in the driver's seat and influencing the outcome of potentially harmful situations. It means starting on the right foot, creating positive synergy and minimizing the need for remedial action later in the project cycle. Looking at conflict management proactively can substantially boost the project team's chances for completing the project successfully.

Planning as a Solution for Handling Conflict

One way to manage conflict is to wait for it to happen and then smother it with a barrage of tactical skills and personal talent. For this approach to be successful, project team members must be well versed in conflict resolution and constantly on the alert for eruptions of dissidence.

Another route to managing conflict, however, is through the *preventive planning approach.* The idea is to allow or set the stage for "beneficial" conflicts while avoiding or eliminating harmful ones. Mapping out sound project moves and making them at the right time will enable the task of wrestling with major crises to be substantially reduced. Although both preventive and corrective measures are needed to deal with conflict, planning is the key to keeping conflict at manageable levels. Here are some ways planning facilitates the task:

♦ *Project planning.* Most project discord emanates from the very basics of project management. Schedules, project priorities, and manpower resources are the primary conflict sources, followed by technical, administrative, and cost objectives. Therefore, if project planning and scheduling functions are properly performed, the odds for meeting project-control parameters are increased and conflict levels tend to diminish.

♦ *Integrative planning.* A "softer" size-up of project conflict pinpoints behavioral characteristics as the primary source. Communication barriers, conflicts of interest, and differences in managerial philosophy are the causes of conflict according to this view. This aspect of conflict can also be managed through planning. If "blended" properly, project teams can be prepared to deal with conflicts on a routine basis. When blending techniques such as those outlined in Chapter 4 are stirred into a "project integration plan," the project team's capacity for dealing with conflict is substantially increased.

♦ *The planning process.* In managing conflict, *how* projects are planned may prove to be more important than the plan itself. By *involving* participants in the planning process, personal commitment is generated. This "consensus" approach, as detailed in Chapter 5, although sometimes both awkward and drawn out, tends to result in a unified plan that consequently produces an implementation phase with lower conflict. This lower conflict level occurs because the potential differences are thrashed out during the planning stage when project resources are not yet fully committed.

Conclusion

Both the project manager and key team members must manage conflict. The dynamic nature of projects requires that substantial management time be dedicated to this task. In some cases, disputes may be settled by a straightforward decision. Most often, however, project managers and team members must bring conflicting parties together and influence them—through a combination of persuasion, pushing, and patience—to make the right project moves.

Good conflict managers work the "front end" of conflict. They size up possible clashes before "contact" is actually made and they work out appropriate action plans to handle potential troubles. They remove barriers and concentrate on both the "hard" objective sources of conflict and the corresponding "soft" behavioral side. They concentrate efforts on building an atmosphere designed to avoid unfruitful conflicts and deal with routine friction as it appears. Talented conflict managers have the ability both to handle conflict when it surfaces and to instigate it when it is appropriate to trigger dissidence that will ultimately result in project benefit.

References

1. Hans J. Thamhain and David L. Wilemon, "Conflict Management in Project Life Cycles," *Sloan Management Review,* vol. 16, no. 3 (Spring 1975), pp. 32–33.
2. Hans J. Thamhain and David L. Wilemon, "Conflict Management in Project-Oriented Work Environments," *Project Management Institute Proceedings* (Washington, D.C., September 1974), p. 88.
3. Adapted from Paul A. Orleman, "General Observations on Conflict in Project Management," *Project Management* (New York: AMR International, 1982), p. PO-49.
4. Alan C. Filley, *Interpersonal Conflict Resolution* (Chicago: Scott, Foresman, 1975), pp. 4–7.
5. Robert R. Blake and Jane S. Mouton, *The Managerial Grid®* (Houston: Gulf Publishing, 1964), and application by Hans J. Thamhain and David L. Wilemon, "Conflict Management in Project Life Cycles," *Sloan Management Review,* vol. 16, no. 3 (Spring 1975), pp. 31–50.
6. Nicki S. Kirchof and John R. Adams, *Conflict Management for Project Managers* (Drexel Hill, Pa.: Project Management Institute, October 1982), p. 42.

7. Kenneth Thomas, "Conflict and Conflict Management," in *Handbook of Industrial and Organizational Psychology*, Marvin D. Dunnette, ed. (Chicago: Rand McNally, 1976), p. 900.
8. Adapted from class notes taken during workshop presentation by Allan R. Cohen at PMI/INTERNET Joint Symposium, Boston, Mass., September 27, 1981.

Chapter 10

Communication

I know that you believe you understand what you think I said, but I am not sure you realize that what you heard is not what I meant.

Anonymous

The Understanding Gap

In *The Little Prince*, Antoine de Saint Exupéry picturesquely describes his frustration as a child when he showed grown-ups his "Drawing Number One" depicting a boa constrictor swallowing an elephant. No one interpreted his picture correctly. In spite of his search for a "true person of understanding," each seemingly clear-sighted adult who saw the drawing would say, "That is a hat."

Since no one could understand his picture, which to him was perfectly clear, he changed his approach. He explained, "Then I would never talk to that person about boa constrictors, or primeval forests, or stars. I would bring myself down to his level. I would talk to him about bridge, and golf, and politics, and neckties. And the grown-up would be greatly pleased to have met such a sensible man."[1]

This early-life "understanding gap" described by Saint Exupéry reflects the frustration set off by poor communication. It also highlights the subsequent need to devise a language intelligible to the audience being addressed. From childhood, humans struggle to make others understand their ideas. The problem starts early and continues through life.

The quality of communication affects every human endeavor. Personal relationships depend on effective communication. Business and professional ties, which are based on relationships between people, are no less dependent.

Project work is particularly susceptible to communication problems. Considering the special characteristics of projects—including overlapping areas of responsibility, blurry lines of authority, complex organizational forms, and inherent conflict—it's no wonder communication skills are put to the test. The complex project atmosphere makes it tough for interpersonal communication to get off to a good start, and once ineffective communication has occurred, future efforts may be blocked by barriers that obstruct the free flow of information.

In project management, communication stands out as a topic of special importance. Professional papers have addressed the topic as it applies specifically to project management. Some authors see communication as the key to integration and the pathway for achieving interpersonal commitment. Others take the view that effective project communication can be reached through quantitative planning, management information systems, and computer graphics. According to authors of other papers, matrix organizations require special communication abilities. Planning and control tools, such as the work breakdown structure, are also shown to be a valuable framework for reciprocal communications.

Overview of Communication Theory

Project communication features distinct yet partially overlapping events. The sender, or source, triggers the process by conceiving an idea. That idea is encoded into language or symbols that effectively describe it. The description is relayed to the receiver. The receiver hears or sees the message, decodes it, and attempts to imagine the idea as originally conceived by the sender.

Communication is an indirect process. As opposed to a crisp, clear transmission of concepts from A to B, it is actually a series of sometimes-faltering steps requiring constant attention to ensure continuity. The sender must clearly conceive the idea, adequately translate it into an appropriate code or language, transmit it neatly through the right media, and monitor the receiver's decoding effort. In this complex procedure, the possibility of communication failure is considerable. First, the transmitter may not conceive the idea clearly, thus passing along a foggy concept, which may subsequently snowball into an increasingly garbled message and finally result in very poor communication—and a perplexed receiver. More commonly, however, the idea burns brightly in the mind of the conceiver, but is encoded poorly. This means that inadequate phrases, figures, or gestures are used to convey the message. In other words, something breaks down between the original thought and actual transmission. What might be generically termed noise or interference also makes its contribution to communication failings. Noise is channel interference that distorts signals. Examples are traffic sounds, the ringing of a phone, and someone passing by or opening a door while communication is taking place. Faulty reception is the final source of communication problems. It may occur because the receiver decodes the message improperly and fails to understand it, even though it may have been conceived, encoded, and transmitted effectively through a noiseless medium. The receiver may simply be a poor listener, or his attitude, goals, or prior experiences may distort the incoming message to conform to what he would like to see or hear.

Feedback

For the sender to discover whether the original message was received, the communication process must be reversed. This calls for feedback—the return path of the communication circuit. In feedback, the receiver transmits signals back to the original sender so that the sender can determine whether the message was correctly received.

In the feedback loop the receiver becomes the sender, encoding the message as it is understood, then transmitting it back through the media to be subsequently decoded. In this final step, the original sender compares the initial concept with the message bounced back through the feedback loop to evaluate the compatibility of the two and the subsequent need for communicating additional clarifications or complementary data.

Feedback must be objective to be useful. Distorted or biased feedback only confuses the sender. Effective feedback gives the sender a clear indication that the message was received and simultaneously pinpoints cloudy issues. Nodding one's head and saying "I understand" are weak forms of feedback. More helpful are full responses such as, "You mean we should draft a new procedure for maintaining field vehicles and show it to you by noon on Tuesday? Do you want to include passenger vehicles in the procedure as well?" Feedback on content is fundamental so that senders can be sure they have, in fact, communicated and not simply attempted to transmit a message.

The need for two-way communication, as opposed to one-way transmission, is illustrated by an experiment in which a geometric figure—a combination of interconnecting rectangles—is described verbally, first using one-way transmission and, in a second case, two-way communication. In both cases, the transmitters are not allowed to show the figure to the receivers. In the first case, the transmitter sends the message in a monologue and receives no verbal feedback, remaining unaware of whether the receivers understand the message or not. In another setting, a second communicator describes the same set of rectangles to another set of receivers, using two-way communication. In this second experiment the receivers are permitted to interrupt, ask questions, and clear up doubts.

In comparing the results of one-way versus two-way communication, two-way communication invariably yields more accurate results. More receivers are able to draw the original geometric figure in the group allowing feedback than in the one-way communication group. Feedback enhances the effectiveness of a communication technique.[2]

Despite the advantages, however, a two-way approach has some drawbacks. It can be noisy and disorderly, with the slowest person holding up the others. The one-way message, on the other hand, appears neat and straightforward, but the communication is less efficient. So while feedback takes time and disturbs the order of communication, in the final analysis, it boosts overall accuracy.

Causes of Ineffective Communication

Why is it that ideas aren't transmitted and received more effectively? Why is a well-intended message sometimes met with stony silence or misinterpreted? Royce A. Coffin, in *The Communicator,* says, "Many people are just plain lazy when it comes to communicating. They may work very hard at their profession, but if they have developed sloppy habits or poor attitudes about getting [their ideas] across to other people, they are not collecting all the rewards."[3] Coffin seems to imply that senders are always at fault. They are lazy, inept, poor planners, and/or poor communicators. If they (the senders) worked at it, the receiving parties would easily understand.

In contrast, Saint Exupéry's example of the communication gap implies that *others* (grown-ups) are the problem. Grown-ups should be able to understand that "Drawing Number One" is a boa constrictor swallowing an elephant. In this view the receiving party has the obligation to perceive correctly the message being transmitted.

Or is communication indeed a two-way problem? Here are samples of communication "twists" to which both sides of the process are susceptible:

+ Differing perceptions regarding goals and objectives of the overall system

* Differing perceptions of the scope and goals of the organization's subsystems
* Competition for facilities, equipment, materials, manpower, and other resources
* Personal antagonisms or personality conflicts between managers and/or other personnel
* Resistance to change on the part of individuals or organizational units[4]

Types of Communication

The form, or combination of forms, for getting a message across is important only as far as it influences the effectiveness of a communication effort. A written note or nod of agreement may be adequate in some cases. Extensive one-on-one discussion, major group meetings, or formal reports may be more appropriate in other situations.

Both spoken and nonspoken types of communication are found in project management. Nonspoken forms that are especially common in project management are corporal (body language), written, dictated, computerized, and graphic. The different forms of spoken and nonspoken communication are utilized alone or, more commonly, in concert. How they are used depends on the situation and on personal style. Communicating effectively is analogous to playing a good game of tennis. The player not only must have style, but must know when and where to use each of several different strokes. Allowances can be made for personal preference—for instance, a steady ground-stroker versus an aggressive net player—yet the player without a complete store of strokes will remain at a disadvantage. Effective communicators must also have an array of communicating "strokes" to be used in accordance with each situation.

Spoken Communication

Project team members express their ideas and thoughts throughout the workday. This occurs typically in transmitting instructions and orientation on a one-on-one basis, in small groups, or at formal meetings. Much of the "project hum" comes from spoken interaction between team members as they grapple with problems and work at accomplishing specific project tasks.

The ability to articulate is a strong advantage in spoken communication. It requires that the sender form a clear concept, pick the proper words, and deliver them with punch. Inarticulate efforts may result in forming apparently profound phrases which, when read with care, prove to be utterly meaningless. For example, try to figure out what former presidential aide Ron Ziegler meant to communicate in this statement:

> You should not interpret by my use of "least unlikely" that ultimately, or when the final decision is made, that that may not be the decision, but what I am saying is that it is only one of the matters under consideration and the decision has not been made.[5]

Communication includes both spoken and nonspoken communication, both what is said and how it is said. Self-expression is strongly influenced by factors other than a sequence of words. These factors are voice, tone, volume, body language, and eye contact. (The last two factors are covered later in this chapter.)

* *Tone of voice.* Tone of voice carries its own messages, such as conviction or insecurity, enthusiasm or depression. The right words sent in the wrong tone will be lost en route to the receiver. Adequately modulated volume calls attention to your message and demands attention. Tone also suggests firmness, strength, authenticity, and a belief in what you're saying.
* *Volume.* Steady-volumed messages become monotonous. Changes help keep the audience's attention. Appropriate volume sends a message that what you say is important and needs attention.

In the project world, spoken communication takes place in markedly distinct forms, each with its own characteristics and restrictions. These are summarized in Table 10-1.

Taped messages and speeches are both forms of one-way communication; they are limited by lack of feedback. Telephone and radio communications allow for two-way information flow, yet are limited by potential channel noise and lack of visibility. The one-on-one dialog is a potentially effective communication form, but it's only good for communicating with one other person. Meetings, which take place in a controlled, multidirectional atmosphere, also use spoken communication, yet are highly dependent on effective leadership. Audio visual forms are enhanced by the visual dimension, but are limited by lack of feedback.

What the Receiver Can Do in Spoken Communication

To improve communication, as a starting point, the receiver can *listen*—which signifies considerably more than

Table 10-1. Samples of spoken communication forms used in project management.

Type of Spoken Message	Characteristic	Restrictions
Taped message	One-way, can be played back.	Lacks feedback and visual emphasis.
Telephone	Two-way.	Lacks visual emphasis (body and facial language).
Shortwave radio	Two-way, intermittent.	Sometimes noisy, lacks visual emphasis.
One-on-one dialog	Two-way.	Only one other person gets the message.
Formal speech	One-way.	Lacks feedback.
Problem-solving meeting	Multidirectional, controlled.	Strongly dependent on leadership and group dynamics.
Video tape, training films, etc.	One-way, audio visual.	Lacks feedback.

just hearing sounds. It means decoding and analyzing what is being transmitted. As Epictetus said, "Nature has given to man one tongue, but two ears, that we may hear from others twice as much as we speak."[6]

Accomplished listeners are active receivers. They listen with their eyes, facial expressions, and body as well as with their ears. They "empathize" with nonspoken messages saying "I'm with you" to the sender. Active listeners nudge their senders silently in quest of further clarification. They also formalize feedback by questioning or commenting so that the sender can determine if the message has suffered distortion. "Shut up and listen!" is about as incoherent a statement as any manager can make. The characteristics of poor and good listeners are summarized here:

The Poor Listener	The Good Listener
Always interrupts.	Looks at me while I'm speaking.
Jumps to conclusions.	
Finishes my sentences.	Questions me to clarify what I'm saying.
Is inattentive; has wandering eyes and poor posture.	Shows concern by asking questions about my feelings.
Changes the subject.	Repeats some of the things I say.
Writes everything down.	
Doesn't give any response.	Doesn't rush me.
Is impatient.	Is poised and emotionally controlled.
Loses temper.	Reacts responsibly with a nod of the head, a smile, or a frown.
Fidgets with pen, pencil, or paper clip nervously.	Pays close attention.
	Doesn't interrupt me.
	Keeps on the subject till I've finished my thoughts.[7]

Nonspoken Communication

Nonspoken communication includes the forms discussed in the sections that follow. Each form can be used in one-way or two-way communication and jointly with spoken forms.

Body Language

As demonstrated in the text on spoken communication, it's hard to separate spoken forms from some other types of communication. In fact, there are those who contend that *words* are of little importance in spoken communication. Perhaps this accounts for the feeling that "something is lacking" when contact is not face-to-face. As an example, important subjects calling for full communication are rarely handled over the phone, because complete communication takes place only when punctuated with other forms of expression.

Unlike words, body language, which includes facial expression, is always "turned on." The body incessantly transmits messages. Even if they're not received consciously by others, the messages are taken in subliminally. Our physical bearing, for example, provides a clue as to whether we're "up" or "down." It communicates pride, confidence, sadness, well-being, or concern. A doubtful facial twinge shrinks powerful words to insignificant murmurings. Smiles sparkle and brighten up the immediate surroundings, while frowns cast a cloud of gray. Body language thus adds to both the content and the flair of the communication process.

Not all agree, however, that body language is important. Says Chester L. Karrass in *Give and Take*, a book on negotiation, "Body language is a kind of home-brewed mish-mash consisting of 90 percent common sense and baloney and 10 percent science." He believes the importance of body language has been highly overrated, yet concedes that when people are unsure or have mixed feelings about given situations, people, or ideas, tension and indecision may set off a search for reassurance, causing people to "stroke their chin, rub their face, play with their arms, legs, or head." He also cautions that, just as people can tell lies with words, they can also use deceptive body language.[8]

While the degree of impact body language has on the communication process is debatable, it is generally agreed that it has a strong influence. Whatever that influence may be, the fundamental conclusion remains that body language is a significant communication channel for which both a sending and a receiving awareness should be developed. A list of common body language signals and interpretations is given as follows:

Body Language	Interpretation
Hand rubbing	Expectation
Clenched fists or crossed arms	Defensive attitude
Leaning back, hands behind head	Superiority
Leaning forward	Interest
Concealing mouth with hands	Uncertainty about words
Scratching head or face	Uncertainty[9]

Written Communication

Managerial style strongly influences written communication practices. Some project managers shy away from written documents, preferring to operate more informally. Others attempt to stake down all project activities with documents. Management style influences both the frequency of written communication and the formality of the documents that result.

Regardless of style, however, written documents are a necessary part of conducting project business. And if documents are clear, concise, and communicative, project goals will be advanced. If not, work may suffer drastic and devastating detours while communication gaps are being patched up.

Although a project manager's options for written communication may run the gamut from simple notes to detailed procedures and instructions, there are common pointers for communicating effectively in most types of writing. "Get to the point" and "keep it simple" are pertinent rules for all types of business and professional writing. Stating the objectives first, then communicating the message in clear language, is a sure way to get your idea across. If the subject involves extensive detail, a concluding "wrap-up" helps reinforce the message.

Managers meet their writing needs in various ways. Some prepare notes or rough drafts in longhand for subsequent typing. Others prefer to dictate to a secretary or an assistant. Electronic dictation, or talking into a dictating machine, is another alternative. Or managers may delegate the writing task to someone else.

Project writing, however, is not limited to conventional correspondence alone. On some projects the volume of written documents may be stupefying. Aside from memos and letters, a barrage of surveys, manuals, reports, specifications, and studies are required. On projects involving several foreign languages and complex logistics, a communications expert may be required to ensure that principles of clear written communication are built into the project management system and that messages are lost neither in the translation nor in the routing. Here are some tips for selected project documents:

- *Studies and surveys.* If studies are numerous, require a standardized format to improve readability.
- *Specifications.* Examine existing norms. Establish additional norms as necessary.
- *Progress reports.* Use a reporting outline; have it reviewed for readability and content.
- *Letters.* Use a model format. Establish policy on word usage and circulate writing pointers to principal letter writers. Fix editing policy with typing pool.
- *Memos and notes.* Encourage use of handwritten two-way memos.

In most projects there are two types of particularly effective written documents. First are those prepared on a preliminary basis and then circulated "for comments." These documents communicate basic concepts and, as contributions and comments are gathered from others, they garner support.

The second type is a document that confirms an agreement. In this case, understanding already exists and the document registers the agreement for reference and information purposes. In both cases, the documents are part of *two-way* communication processes.

One-way writings can also be effective, but the challenge is far greater. One-way written communication on topics that are not handled simultaneously through other channels (telephone discussions, meetings, conversations) must be *absolutely* clear. The written communication must paint a picture so sharp and vibrant it can't possibly be misinterpreted. And if action is required, the words must motivate the receiver to act. This is a large task for mere words arranged on a piece of paper.

Dictation

As mentioned earlier, dictation provides a means for managers to meet their writing needs. Dictation is a quick way to get thoughts on record or to pass along information and instructions that, in final form, will be in writing. Although the dictation process includes the element of speech, it is considered nonspoken because of its emphasis on the written product.

Aside from pointing out the evident time-saving advantages of dictation, Auren Uris, author of *Mastering the Art of Dictation*, states that, "People who master the ability to dictate will find they 'write' more fluently, more freely, and more effectively, and express their thoughts more cogently than those who seek to put the same ideas down on paper directly."[10] In other words, dictation helps channel a natural flow of ideas, making the ultimate message more readable. It helps the communicator plow past jargon and get the message across in plain language. Winston Churchill was a believer in straightforward communication—and reacted strongly when criticized for ending a sentence with a preposition. His laconic response was: "This is the type of arrant pedantry up with which I shall not put."[11] Since the time of Churchill's protest, writing rules have been relaxed, particularly in business, where the prime concern is to get the message across. The use of a "dictating language" for letters, memos, and Telexes has caused written language to take on some of the characteristics of spoken communication. Within this framework, grammatical minutiae are subordinated to the task of clearly communicating the message—a trend that would surely have pleased Winston Churchill.

Dictating is simply a different way of transmitting a message. It comes easily for some people; for others, it constitutes a long, slow learning process. But pay-offs in communication speed offer an enticing reward for learning to write out loud. Dictation can be used as a major communication tool or as a supplement to conventional writing. Here are sample applications:

- *Communicating with yourself.* Put reminders and follow-up items on tape.
- *Sending messages to a secretary or assistant.* Dictate routine communications instead of interrupting your staff members. They can listen to your taped instructions at their convenience.
- *Preparing letters or memos.* Use your machine for dictating routine correspondence.
- *Outlining major reports.* Start the first draft or outline of a major document by dictating the topics and primary content.
- *Drafting and rehearsing presentations.* Prepare and polish presentations by dictating.

Other Nonspoken Forms of Project Communication

Project communication takes on still other nonspoken forms, such as computerized and graphic. To what extent each of the following forms is used depends largely on the type of project.

- *Computerized data processing (CDP).* Although still plagued to some extent by the "garbage in, garbage out" syndrome and poor report readability, CDP has become an effective communication tool. People have learned how to deal more effectively with computers. Computer design has shown an increased sensitivity to human limitations. Managers have also realized that only a small portion of what is processed should actually reach the final user's eyes.

• *Electronic mail.* Electronic mail puts correspondence on the manager's office display screen for subsequent instructions, which can be instantly punched into the computer. The display can be held for reference while dictating or keying in a response. Electronic mail can substantially cut down the project paper parade.

• *Computer graphics.* Because many laypersons and managers find text-based computer reports hard to read, computer graphics present a solution to "spruce up" presentations. Networks and many other graphic representations can be produced by computers so users can "see" rather than read the message. CAD/CAE/CAM approaches (computer-aided design/computer-aided engineering/computer-aided manufacturing) also contain computer graphics aimed primarily at the calculating, design, and drafting functions.

• *Design drawings and sketches.* Whether computerized or not, this form constitutes the communications crux of most technologically based projects. Drawings, consisting of symbols, lines, and words, establish what the project is all about. Standards exist for most types of engineering drafting. Communicability in engineering drawings is closely linked to adherence to standard drafting norms.

Key to Communication Effectiveness: Planning

Communication, like all interactive efforts, flows more smoothly if good planning precedes actual performance. Formal communications may require more preparation than the informal, but when the stakes are high, any type of communication must be carefully thought out in advance. Major communication gaps loom when there is a lack of appropriate planning. There is little justification for the occurrence of most major communication problems—almost any situation can be planned for. The following list indicates the planning required for each type of communication.

- *Formal presentation.* Prepare outline, complete text, critique, rehearse.
- *Telephone call.* List all topics to be discussed. (If the person isn't there, can someone else handle the subject?)
- *Letters and memos.* Outline objectives, prepare proper slant, dictate.
- *One-on-one dialog.* Establish purpose of encounter. Use tailor-made approach for each type of person (different strokes for different folks).
- *Meetings.* Fix objectives and agenda topics. Decide what props or additional data are required. Prepare minutes.

Exactly how much planning is needed may vary substantially. An unusually articulate project manager may get by with a sketchy plan for, say, convincing the client that "the lost schedule time will be made up within 60 days." A more methodical and less articulate manager, however, might have to delve into considerable detail, prepare back-up data, and promote preliminary conversations to boost the chances of getting the message across. Planning, therefore, improves the probability of success in any situation and can also help offset other communication shortcomings.

Sketching Out the Communication Plan

All important communications require planning—even those that appear straightforward. Proper planning can make the difference between selling an idea and seeing it ignored or pushed aside. A back-of-envelope approach outlining simple steps is often adequate. Here's a sample communication plan for selling a new idea to upper management:

- *Send advance warning.* Before approaching superiors (or whoever must approve the idea) with detailed justification, send a note with brief supporting data as a device for "testing the waters."
- *Use expert opinion.* Find someone who wrote or said something about the subject. Use it as support. Superiors sometimes reject bright ideas from their subordinates because they, the superiors, weren't consulted previously. An outside expert's view makes a new idea more palatable.
- *Garner support.* Create general awareness of the subject by circulating copies of a related article, graph, or illustration so others can be exposed to the idea.
- *Be patient.* Don't let your enthusiasm make you overanxious. Relax and wait for the right moment.
- *Give more information.* After briefly discussing the subject with upper management, submit more information and suggestions in draft form. Await comments.
- *Negotiate.* Incorporate comments and discuss the subject regarding further preliminary action.

Once barriers to communication have been hurdled and feedback is generated, the subject can be dealt with in a straightforward manner. Planning is needed, however, to ensure that communication starts out on the right foot and is not cut off before the message gets a fair hearing.

Conclusion

How can a picture of a boa constrictor swallowing an elephant be interpreted as a hat? In *The Little Prince*, these two sharply differing perceptions constitute a common form of misunderstanding often labeled the "communication gap." Saint Exupéry changes his communicating technique when he discovers that the receivers' form of processing information is different from his own. Upon sizing up the negative feedback sparked by his communication attempts, he changes his approach and begins to talk of "bridge, golf, politics, and neckties."

Since people are unique, each individual's "information processor" is different. While some techniques may be common to people of similar backgrounds, age groups, and nationalities, each person's reasoning process retains a certain individuality. It's as if each mind were a computer, with similarities to others, but with minor differences in programming. For one human computer to communicate with any other means either devising a common program, operable and understood by all, or being sufficiently graphic and visual so the message can actually be translated by each individual's computer.

In the case of human beings, devising a common program is often done through drilling and training. This leads individuals to perceive a more or less universal view. In this common-program mode, for instance, upon hearing the words "navy blue," all trained receivers would conjure up visions of a common hue. In the other mode, calling for "clear and graphic representation," navy blue must be *shown* so that individuals can process the information in accordance with their personal programs.

In communication, care must be taken to respect people's individualities, including each person's unique method of processing information. If such care is taken, most any message can be communicated effectively. Even "Drawing Number One" can evoke the response, "That's a boa constrictor swallowing an elephant," if the proper groundwork is laid.

References

1. Antoine de Saint Exupéry, *The Little Prince* (New York: Harcourt Brace Jovanovich, 1971), p. 5.
2. Harold J. Leavitt, *Managerial Psychology* (Chicago: University of Chicago Press, 1975), pp. 114–124.
3. Royce A. Coffin, *The Communicator* (New York: AMACOM, 1975), p. viii.

4. Linn C. Stuckenbruck, "The Job of the Project Manager: Systems Integration," *The Implementation of Project Management: The Professional's Handbook* (Reading, Mass.: Addison-Wesley, 1981), p. 152.
5. Nigel Rees, ed., *Quote . . . Unquote* (New York: St. Martin's Press, 1979), p. 79.
6. As quoted in Robert L. Montgomery, *Listening Made Easy* (New York: AMACOM, 1981), p. 13.
7. *Ibid.*, pp. 14–15.
8. Chester L. Karrass, *Give and Take* (New York: Thomas Y. Crowell, 1974), pp. 16–18.
9. Gerard I. Nierenberg and Henry H. Calero, *How to Read a Person Like a Book* (New York: Hawthorn Books, 1971), pp. 20, 21, 41, 44, 67, 107, 150, 165.
10. Auren Uris, *Mastering the Art of Dictation* (Houston, Tex.: Gulf Publishing, 1980), p. 3.
11. As quoted in Rudolf Flesch, *How to Write, Speak, and Think More Effectively* (New York: Harper & Row, 1951), p. 92.

Chapter 11

Negotiating

Successful negotiators are like skilled fencers.
They thrust, parry, retreat, pause, feint, and attack—and throughout the match take special
care to protect their sensitive areas.

Work, Life, and Negotiation

Negotiating is a part of everyone's daily life. People jockey
for position and strive to improve their situations by negotiating "contracts" with those around them. These contracts establish working relationships and fix, either casually
or formally, terms of agreement. Negotiating, therefore, is a
natural and inevitable consequence of human behavior.

The need to develop negotiating skills appears to be on
the rise in all areas of human endeavor. As conflict-prone
situations proliferate and people want to participate more
in making the decisions that affect their lives, more and
more occasions call for negotiation. They reject or subcon-
sciously sabotage decisions dictated by others. Since people
often hold different views, it takes *negotiation* to conciliate
the differences.

Negotiation in Project Management

Major projects are fertile fields for negotiation. For instance, reaching agreement on the project's prime contracts requires negotiation. Claims are settled through negotiation, as are numerous daily project situations that involve push-pull parrying with others. Some organizational forms such as the matrix introduce a need for special "horizontal" bargaining skills. Throughout the project's life cycle, there is a constant demand for negotiation among the project team, owners, joint venture partners, financing agencies, and other parties with vested interests in the project's completion. The following require negotiating skills:

- *Contracts.* Most major projects feature a web of interrelated contracted services and obligations. Prime contracts and special service contracts are samples of such negotiated agreements.
- *Procurement.* Materials and equipment acquisition is another area commonly open to negotiation. Price and delivery are usually the focus of such dealings.
- *"In-house" negotiation.* In horizontal or matrix organizations, informal in-house negotiation takes place on a routine basis because most project problems are managed by striking negotiated agreements.
- *Negotiation with third parties.* Ongoing contacts with third parties such as clients, government agencies, or contractors also require artful negotiation for resolving conflicts.
- *Claims and contract close-out.* Contractors typically present claims for cost increases when they believe certain work was performed in excess of the original scope agreed to, or when conditions under which work was performed are considered different from initial premises.

Negotiation Classified by Results

As in conflict resolution, there are three possible negotiation outcomes: (1) win-win, (2) win-lose, and (3) lose-lose. Since negotiation is a form of conciliating conflictive positions, natural parallels exist between conflict management and negotiation.

Win-Win Negotiation

In win-win situations, both negotiating parties are satisfied with the results. A win-win negotiation might be exemplified by a vendor who sells quality wares to an industrial buyer at a competitive yet profitable price. For the seller, the deal is expected to yield a reasonable return; the buyer in turn looks forward to receiving a quality product at the prearranged price and within a fixed time frame.

For make-to-order contracts calling for future delivery of goods or services, win-win deals are of particular importance. Upon signing the contract, the buyer actually purchases a promise that quality goods or services will be delivered within the specified time frame. The buyer, who deals from an apparently powerful negotiating position, is thus really purchasing hope, because the product and/or service will only be delivered later. If the contract is not struck on a win-win basis, one party may lose and subsequently affect the other's apparent win position. Win-win negotiation is the crucial rule of thumb for relationships that are ongoing, whether they are of a business or personal nature.

Win-Lose Negotiation

Win-lose outcomes are characterized by two polarized parties: the "victor" and the "vanquished." In the case of ongoing relationships, this presents a prickly situation; the defeated party will try to "get even" if given a chance. For one-time deals, however, such as site acquisition for a new factory, such a harsh negotiting method is justified. In this case, the buying party takes immediate possession of the property and is unlikely to deal with the seller in the future. Reprisals aren't probable since the purchaser assumes legal domination over the acquired land. In this type of situation each side generally tends to bring out heavy bargaining guns in order to make gains at the negotiating table, often to the serious detriment of the opposing party.

Lose-Lose Negotiation

Lose-lose negotiation outcomes result when one or both parties take such an extreme position that no deal is struck at all and both parties' propositions are deflated. Lose-lose situations may also result from negotiations that at first appear to lean toward a "win-lose" stance. A hard-struck contract for fixed-price construction, for instance, can become a double-loser if the contracting party takes advantage of a financially hard-pressed builder at contract-signing time. A tough deal may come back to haunt the hard-nosed negotiator when it later becomes apparent that the builder will be unable to perform or simply loses interest in the job.

A classic example is depicted by the protracted round of negotiations between New York City newspapers and the city's printers' unions back in the early 1960s. The unions drove a hard bargain and achieved unprecedented contract benefits and sizable wage boosts. Unfortunately, the unions ended up negotiating themselves partially out of business, since many of the papers were simply unable to hold up under the stiff financial terms imposed. Newspapers either merged or folded, leaving weakened enterprises and fewer jobs for union members. This type of negotiation corresponds to the situation where the physician declares, "The operation was a success, but the patient died."

The Art and Science of Negotiation

Negotiation, like project management, is both an art and a science. Meeting the challenge depends partly on natural talent and the ability to use behavioral skills. The rest depends on planning, organizing, and follow-through. Because negotiations are handled by human beings, not by computers or robots, they are substantially influenced by the participants' emotions, values, backgrounds, and viewpoints. Unlike robots, people are often unpredictable. They may not react as they "should," particularly when placed in the highly interactive and visible negotiating arena. This means that the "people side" of negotiating requires constant attention. Negotiating partners must be sized up: their psyches, personality profiles, and underlying values must be thoroughly evaluated early on.

The "art" side of negotiation is affected by the *human chemistry* involved. Negotiation is always colored by behavioral influences such as personality, sense of timing, empathy, listening skills, and ability to articulate. Such variables can't be plugged into a computer or put into a formula. Human relationships are simply too complex to program. Since human beings are moved by both logic and emotion, rational approaches may not prevail during negotiation. The art of negotiating thus requires an inherent perception of the behavioral subtleties involved in striking a deal.

The other side of successful negotiation is both rational and scientific. It involves basic *negotiation planning*, which can readily be pursued on an orderly and organized basis. Simple questions lay the groundwork for the negotiation plan, which is designed to serve as a guideline throughout the bargaining process. Here are the types of questions that should be answered in the negotiation plan: What is my negotiating agenda? What items can we give up? What are our strong and weak points? What roles will be played by the members of my negotiating team? What negotiating sequence shall we use? What is our bottom line?

Training both experienced and neophyte bargainers can also be done scientifically. Through formal training, negotiators can test skills and upgrade performance through systematic exposure to basic techniques, tips, and tactics. Although planning and training won't make mediocre negotiators into master arbiters, the performance of those who lack sufficient exposure to the basic negotiating skills can be boosted substantially by applying scientific methods.

Hard, Soft, and "Yes" Negotiation

When negotiating, most people find themselves in dilemmas because they lean too far toward one of two extreme bargaining approaches: either the "soft" or the "hard" way. In "soft" negotiation, conflict tends to be avoided while sensitivity to personal feelings runs high. The soft approach is characterized by friendly negotiations, where the principal goal is to *agree* so that the relationship can be maintained even at the cost of heavy concessions. This "soft touch" reaches both the people and the problem. It is based on openness and trust, and often ultimately results in a tendency to yield under pressure in order to reach agreement.

The "hard" school brings a tough, unshakable line to the negotiating table. Positions are set in concrete and the participants are seen as adversaries. The goal is to win at all costs with little concern for the well-being of the other party. The hard line is also applied to both the problem and the people. Demands are made in a climate of extreme distrust. The objective is to achieve one-sided gains through hard-line, high-pressure tactics.

There is a third way to negotiate—a way that brings out the best of both the hard and soft schools. The "Harvard Negotiating Project" proposes that questions be negotiated on their merits rather than having participants engage in a "haggling process focused on what each side says it will and won't do." Mutual gain and fair standards for handling conflict are also considered fundamental. "Hard on merits, and soft on people" sums up the *yes* approach to negotiating. The objective of the method is to arrive at just negotiations based on an atmosphere of mutual fairness. This applies both to the process and to the outcome. The Harvard method, called *principled negotiation*, or *negotiation on merits*, is summarized in the following four points:

People	"Separate the people from the problem."
Interests	"Focus on interests, not positions."

Options	"Generate a variety of possibilities before deciding what to do."
Criteria	"Insist that the results be based on some objective standard."[1]

In principled negotiation, it is assumed that the players are problem solvers and that the objective is to reach a wise outcome, efficiently and amicably. This can be done by being, in effect, easy on the people and tough on the problem. Focusing on interests rather than on positions is also part of principled negotiation and implies fully exploring mutual and divergent interests before trying to converge on some bottom line. The tenet "invent options for mutual gain," calling for a creative search for alternatives, is also held as fundamental by proponents of the Harvard method. Likewise, objective criteria are needed in order to establish standards independent of personal foibles and to fix principles designed to resist pressure.

Phased Negotiation

For analysis purposes, negotiation can be broken into three phases. Each phase, corresponding essentially to before, during, and after negotiation, calls for a specific focus involving a set of actions appropriate for that stage of the process. The phases—prenegotiation, active negotiation, and postnegotiation—are discussed here in detail.

Prenegotiation

Prenegotiation encompasses everything that needs to be prepared or thought out before sitting down at the bargaining table. Examples are planning (both strategic and tactical), fixing priorities, assigning roles, and establishing basic limits to trade-offs and negotiation. In a sense, all these prenegotiation activities can be grouped under the planning label— a proven managerial tool sometimes cast aside in an effort to "get the show on the road." The use or misuse of planning can make or break a negotiation effort. Particularly significant in the prenegotiation stage is the fact that each side can use this stage basically as it sees fit. A negotiating party may prepare either extensively or superficially for an upcoming negotiating bout. Yet the quality of this planning, which precedes stepping into the negotiating ring, is a managerial decision that strongly influences the final outcome of negotiation.

Prenegotiation is aimed at developing an overall strategy. The tactics appropriate for implementing that strategy evolve from a study of both sides' true objectives and a systematic sifting of the facts. Prenegotiation efforts are characterized by information gathering and analysis—and by broad questioning of issues. During prenegotiation, be sure to do the following:

- *Establish overall strategy.* What are the true goals? What negotiating approach will be used? What is a reasonable range within which a deal may be struck? What are appropriate trade-offs?
- *Size up the opponents.* What are the opponents' objectives? What is their possible maximum and minimum position? Where are they strong and where are they weak?
- *Pick the right negotiating team.* Select a "mix" of negotiators able to face the opponent's shrewdest, most capable representatives. Does the team have a clear picture of the technical, economic, and behavioral issues? Is it endowed with due authority?
- *Collect the facts.* Although negotiation is heavily affected by behavioral traits, fundamental fact-collecting must not be neglected. Complex points of engineering, accounting, cost analysis, and business law may be involved. Question whether the facts have been thoroughly analyzed before negotiation begins.

Active Negotiation

Active negotiation begins with the first significant discussion and ends when agreement is reached. This phase includes the activities embodied within the start and finish lines—which may cover a time span of minutes (a brief meeting) or years (international trade agreements). It's during this phase that on-stage action takes place, even though extended periods of inaction may separate the negotiation sessions in some cases. Broad principles governing active negotiation are summarized as follows:

- *Know the facts and figures.* Bring hard facts to the negotiating table and use them with conviction.
- *Guard against emotional reactions.* Avoid being drawn into discussions on emotional grounds; don't be "baited" by opponents.
- *Allow retreat.* Be sensitive to others' face-saving needs; allow the opponents to withdraw gracefully.
- *Make major moves carefully.* Evaluate timing of major moves. Showdowns, offers, and counter-offers should be made when the time is right.
- *Be sensitive to others' emotional needs.* The need of others to be in the limelight, to claim a win, or to be reassured or comforted should be satisfied as much as possible.

During active negotiations, aggressive tactics such as moving in on your opponent, upsetting strategies, and holding back reserves can also be used when the situation calls for it. Here are ways that aggressive negotiating tactics can be applied.

- *Use diversionary tactics.* Bring up trivialities to divert attention from your weaknesses.
- *Reverse the roles.* Anticipate their arguments and use them to strengthen your own position.

- *Overwhelm your opponents.* Take a strong lead and put them on the defensive. Make sure, however, you have calculated the relative strengths correctly.
- *Evade attacks on your weak points.* Swing the debate back to your strengths.
- *Use the shotgun approach.* Scatter out as many negotiating points as possible and demand proof.
- *Draw out frontal attack by opponents.* This applies when your position is stronger; otherwise, their arguments may overpower you.
- *Start out slowly.* After the opponents reveal their position, move in with stronger points. Try to draw out your opponents by discussing your weaker points first.
- *Be secretive.* Don't reveal your true objectives or the concessions you are seeking.
- *Ignore the client's strong points or tricky questions.* Pretend you misunderstand and continue making your points.
- *Purposely create an impasse.* Raise serious complicating factors with your opponent.

Some aggressive approaches, however, fall into the "dirty tricks" department. Dirty tricks are those techniques that constitute a breach of acceptable practices or negotiating ethics. While they seem to result in apparent gains, they may actually set off a "boomerang" effect, particularly if the relationship is ongoing. Fisher and Ury list the following as unethical:

Deliberate deception
Phony facts
Ambiguous authority
Dubious intentions
Less than full disclosure
Psychological warfare
Stressful situations
Personal attacks
The good-guy/bad-guy routine
Threats

Positional pressure tactics
Refusal to negotiate
Extreme demands
Escalating demands
Lock-in tactics
Hardhearted partner
A calculated delay
A "take it or leave it" attitude[2]

Postnegotiation

Once an understanding is reached, the postnegotiation or wrap-up phase begins. The agreement is shaped into a formal pact. Procedural points such as joint statements, press coverage, signatures, and other formalities are part of this "after" phase. Postnegotiation protocol calls for avoiding discussion of the negotiation outcome with opponents and generally steering clear of commenting on relative negotiating abilities.

Once the deal has been "signed, sealed, and delivered," an in-house critique on the effectiveness of the negotiation strategy and performance is appropriate. Finally, feedback on later developments is the ultimate and ongoing part of postnegotiation. It helps the negotiator determine whether the deal was a good one and evaluate techniques that might enhance future negotiations. Postnegotiation involves the following steps:

- *Completing the agreement.* Written details should be worked out promptly in order to characterize the final agreement.
- *Observing protocol.* Avoid discussing the agreement and the relative abilities of the negotiating teams.
- *Obtaining feedback.* Critique negotiations and set up a system for receiving feedback on later developments.

What Makes a Good Negotiator?

The qualities of successful negotiators cover a broad spectrum and may sometimes appear contradictory. Negotiators must be quick, yet patient; articulate, yet good listeners; hard-nosed, yet flexible; unemotional, yet good-humored. They need to be able to size up their opponent's strong and weak points and evaluate the behavioral side of the negotiation. An inherent liking for people, poise, and self-restraint are other qualities required of the negotiator.

Truly great negotiators are probably born, not made. The art of negotiation is such an important part of the game that no amount of scientific planning can fully replace it. Yet, just as a bright stone can be polished to shine even brighter, good negotiators can also better their skills through practice, procedure, and training. By the same token, a less-talented negotiator, like a lower-quality stone, can also be buffed up to an acceptable "shine."

One approach to developing negotiating skills is through the *cognitive process*. By learning the negotiation basics, the would-be negotiator becomes better equipped to enter the bargaining arena. Negotiation planning lends itself particularly to such a didactic approach. Other skills such as active listening and body language, although largely behavioral in nature, can be sharpened as well through cognitive reading techniques.

Other negotiation-related skills such as empathy, sense of timing, creative thinking, and ability to articulate are also dealt with in the professional writings on behavioral management. Skills in these areas can be improved through concentrated cognitive exposure. The principles for successfully managing the behavioral side of negotiating range from being almost tangible to nearly nebulous, making it a difficult art to master. Yet persistence in pursuing new levels of negotiating excellence will surely result in a better success rate at the negotiating table. The following guidelines can help boost negotiating skills:

- Read up on negotiation in management-oriented magazine articles, monographs, books, and professional papers. Establish a quota of, say, one article per week.
- Raise your awareness level by attending a seminar or course on negotiation.

- Choose an area of negotiation that you feel needs special attention. Establish a time frame for practicing that skill.
- Ask others to observe you and critique your technique.
- Polish, practice, and recycle.

Conclusion

Negotiations are, generally, verbal interchanges, which are often ultimately summed up in written form. They depend on planning, accumulating facts, and human interaction. Tangible rewards, ego satisfaction, social contact, creative expression, aggression, need for escape, sense of duty, and personality quirks are also part of the negotiation game. This makes negotiation a strongly people-oriented endeavor. Results are thus heavily affected by the participant's behavior in the before, during, and after phases of project negotiation.

References

1. Roger Fisher and William Ury, *Getting to Yes* (Boston: Houghton Mifflin, 1976), p. xi.
2. *Ibid.*, pp. 137–147.

Chapter 12

Decision Making and Problem Solving

A decision is a judgment. It is a choice between alternatives. It is rarely a choice between right and wrong.

Peter F. Drucker

Making Project Decisions

Making decisions and solving problems are what project management is all about. Decisions cover a sweeping spectrum of problems, including all the whats, whens, wheres, whos, whys, and hows that crop up during the life cycle of the project. Whether large or small, virtually all decisions are made in response to the following questions:

+ What must be done? (Scope and task definition.)
+ When is it required? (Schedule and control.)
+ Where should it be performed? Be built? Be delivered? (Logistics.)
+ Who should do the job? Who should be responsible? (Task assignment.)

♦ Why should it be done this way? (Evaluation.)
♦ How should it be done? (Planning and analysis.)

All project activities focus on decision making in one
form or another. Approval of project plans, which are designed to keep future problems from popping up, call for
carefully wrought decisions. Expediting efforts require another kind of project decision. Data gathering and evaluation
of alternatives are other project activities linked to the decision-making process. Negotiations and ongoing problem
solving represent yet other decision-making tasks.

The project team's mission is to make good decisions
that are designed to result in the "best" solutions. That's
the hard part, of course—trying to come up with the best
response to a project's problems. According to Russell L.
Ackoff in *The Art of Problem-Solving*, opportunities for making decisions, whether project-related or not, exist only under the following circumstances: (1) when there are at least
two available courses of action, (2) when at least two possible
outcomes of unequal value exist, and (3) when the different
available courses have different levels of effectiveness. Choice
exists when the decision maker's action causes a difference
in the value of the outcome.[1]

Before trying to determine the right choice, however,
the problem itself needs to be put into perspective. First,
the problem is viewed by *the group or individual faced with
it.* Second, a problem can be seen through its *controllable
variables*—those aspects over which the decision maker has
influence or control. The third facet of problem evaluation
includes the *uncontrollable variables*—those things that are
completely outside the decision maker's control. These variables may be quantitative or qualitative in nature. Fourth,
problems are exposed to *constraints imposed internally or
externally* by the decision makers themselves or by others
who affect the decision. The fifth and last facet of the problem
involves the *possible outcomes* that are produced by the
combination of the decision maker's choice and the influencing uncontrolled variables.[2]

Problems appear because of a perceived deficiency. They are labeled as such when it becomes obvious to those affected that corrective action is needed. Problems may result from omission or lack of action, faulty or inadequate planning, poorly made prior decisions, or changing or unpredictable conditions. Ackoff suggests that the inability to achieve adequate solutions is largely due to self-imposed constraints unconsciously applied to situations by decision makers. This causes a tunnel-vision approach to problem solving that restricts the number of alternative solutions.[3]

The path to making and carrying out good decisions is strewn with obstacles. Good decision making requires, first, breaking free of constraints, then questioning the information base and process used for reaching the decision, and, finally, adjusting the decision to an ever-changing environment.

The Decision-Making Process

How should decisions be made? What's the best way to go about it? Is there a prescribed step-by-step approach for arriving at the best solution? Simply put, the best decision-making process is the one that works within the context in question. Such a decision can be effective without necessarily being classically correct. If the "correct" solution is ultimately rejected or sabotaged by other parties, it is no solution at all.

Many people do not understand their own decision-making processes, which are hidden away in the subconscious mind like the submerged part of an iceberg. Group decision making can be even more obscure because it involves interactions among several people, who may be more ego-centered than objective and more intuitive than logical. In decision making, being right isn't enough. "Will it work?" is the true test of decisions.

According to some theorists, decisions should be made according to a step-by-step game plan. Others favor a less structured yet equally disciplined approach that requires maintaining a healthy debate until full consensus is reached. In the following text some of these decision-making procedures are examined.

The Kepner-Tregoe (K-T) process focuses on solving problems, or dealing with situations in which what is *actually* happening deviates from what *should* be happening. The process concentrates on sorting out relevant and irrelevant data associated with the problem's cause. The method includes the basic cycles of problem analysis, decision analysis, and potential problem analysis. The system effectively enlarges the decision-making process, making it more visible to the decision maker. This higher visibility coupled with a systematic analytical approach creates an effective problem-solving kit.[4]

Problem Analysis

Problem analysis is the first part of the process. The K-T approach of starting with a detailed problem analysis is consistent with the management axiom: "If you properly identify and understand the problem, you're already halfway to the solution." In problem analysis, the problem analyzer starts with a standard of performance against which progress is measured. Perceived deviations from this standard are used to identify the problem that needs analysis. Then the variance is pinpointed and described in detail. The next step is to analyze "what was affected" versus "what was not affected" by the change. Subsequently the distinctive feature or condition that set off the unwanted effect is identified. Then the possible causes of the deviation are deduced; finally, the deviation's most likely cause is found by matching the possible causes against the problem's specification. Thus, the basic steps of problem analysis are:

1. Establish performance standard.
2. Identify performance deviation.
3. Describe deviation in detail.
4. Analyze distinguishing factor.
5. Identify change caused by distinctive features.

6. Pinpoint possible causes.
7. Identify most likely deviation cause.[5]

The first part of the process attempts to discover the cause through a detailed analysis of the problem itself. The actual cause may be clothed in technical trappings but be behavioral in origin. Step-by-step analysis helps smoke out the real reasons behind the problem. Once the problem has been picked apart and the cause duly pinpointed, the actual decision-making process takes over. In K-T terms, this phase of choosing among the different ways of getting things done is called decision analysis.

Decision Analysis

The process of decision analysis begins by establishing objectives and classifying them in order of importance. Alternatives are then raised and weighed against fixed targets. A tentative choice is singled out and analyzed for adverse consequences, which are taken into consideration in the final decision. Thus, the steps of K-T decision analysis are:

1. Fix objectives.
2. Establish priorities of objectives.
3. Develop alternative solutions.
4. Evaluate alternatives.
5. Make a tentative choice.
6. Test for adversity.
7. Plan against adversity.[6]

This structured procedure helps stave off hip shot decisions. Although the final result is still a "judgment call," it is guided by the logic and discipline of procedure.

Kepner and Tregoe take the process a step further by sizing up problems prior to putting decisions into effect. They call this stage "potential problem analysis."

Potential Problem Analysis

Potential problem analysis begins with an action plan. The potential problems are listed and the risk assessed. Possible causes are identified and their probability of occurrence considered. The remaining steps are aimed at prevention and include sizing up ways to eliminate causes or reduce effects. Finally, priorities are established and a control system is mapped out. The steps for analyzing potential problems are:

1. Develop action plan.
2. List potential problems.
3. Assess risk.
4. Identify causes.
5. Assess probabilities.
6. Establish cause prevention.
7. Fix plan for primary problem.
8. Establish controls.[7]

The two greatest failings of decision makers are (1) providing inadequate definition of problems and their causes and (2) placing insufficient emphasis on searching out alternative solutions. In other words, the first steps in the decision-making process are underplayed. Procedural decision making as prescribed by Kepner and Tregoe persuades decision makers to begin at the beginning.

The Essence of Decision Making

While the K-T approach offers an in-depth procedure for deciding, a simple stripped-down version of the process can be used for handy review and reference. This abbreviated formula draws on long-held management rules regarding decision making. The essence of the decision-making method is contained in the answers to the following classic questions:

- What constitutes the problem and its causes?
- What are the possible alternative solutions?

- What is the "best" solution?
- What is the best way to put it into effect?

Step-by-step decision making, whether simplified or spelled out in detail, offers a procedure for managerial action that is otherwise carried out intuitively. While intuition should not be cast aside, a more structured "road map" approach keeps decision makers from leap-frogging ahead of certain important intermediate steps. It provides a valuable option for the ill-advised decision maker who, armed only with opinions, biases, and self-imposed constraints, makes a few flailing attempts at gathering the facts on a poorly defined problem before boldly proceeding to make the most subjective of decisions.

Deciding the Japanese Way

According to Drucker, "The only people who have developed a systematic and standardized approach to decision making are the Japanese. Their decisions are highly effective. Yet their approach violates every rule in the books on decision making."[8] Why is the Japanese approach for reaching decisions so confusing to Westerners? What makes it so different from North American and European approaches? Drucker says all authorities on Japan concur on one fundamental point: Japanese institutions make decisions by consensus. Only after agreement, or consensus, has been reached is the decision put into effect.

Reaching a consensus, however, is no easy matter. Consensus is achieved only when every participant believes the following:

- "I believe that you understand my point of view."
- "I believe that I understand your point of view."
- "Whether or not I prefer this decision, I will support it because it was arrived at in an open and fair manner."[9]

Although obviously effective in specific cultures, the consensus technique is often criticized as being cumbersome and time-consuming. For instance, it ties up costly personnel while minor details of understanding are worked out. To obtain general agreement means mobilizing everyone who will be involved in carrying out the venture. Each person must analyze the subject individually; together, the group must reach a common conclusion about how the job should be done.

Despite its drawbacks, however, consensus decision making has strong redeeming qualities—starting with the simple fact that, in practice, it is highly effective. The fruits of arduously negotiated agreement pay off in terms of increased productivity, which Ouchi suggests is rooted in worker involvement. In other words, productivity is augmented through the process of intertwining in the decision-making process the parties who will ultimately perform the work. This process, according to Ouchi, also breeds trust and subtlety, which are seen as being intimately connected with productivity.[10]

Consensus decision making, however, is not the exclusive property of the Japanese. Although the "pure" Japanese model, called "Theory J," depends on characteristics inherent to the Japanese culture (including "unselfishness, sense of intimacy, caring, and support"), non-Japanese firms such as Hewlett Packard and Procter & Gamble have applied decision-making processes similar to the Japanese model. The corresponding American model, which shares such Japanese managerial traits as intimacy, subtlety, and trust, is dubbed the "Type Z" organization.[11]

The Japanese consensus system can be incredibly time-consuming. Yet implementation and subsequent decision making become much easier because virtually all the people involved in the venture have *literally* affixed their seal of approval to the agreement. The abbreviated American version of reaching a consensus typically involves fewer people and consequently requires a shorter time period. By extension, implementing the task poses a greater challenge, because others who are to perform the work may have to be "sold" on the project later.

In summary, Japanese decision making is based on the proposition that generalized commitment is required to reach adequate productivity levels. Commitment in turn comes from worker involvement and participation, which is obtained through consensus decision making.

Creativity in the Decision-Making Process

Creativity is of such importance that it might be considered the very essence of problem solving. An example of creative decision making is given in a story that begins with complaints by building tenants about poor elevator service. In an attempt to settle the issue, consultants were brought in by the building manager. The capacity and frequency of elevator service were analyzed in detail. Three alternatives were presented: (1) add elevators, (2) replace some or all of the existing elevators, or (3) add a control system for routing the elevators to yield faster service. All alternatives were extremely expensive when compared with the building's earnings.

In desperation, the building manager called in subordinates and suggested a brain-storming session to generate other ideas not raised by the consultants. Various suggestions were made and put aside. Finally, an unconventional solution blurted out by an assistant from the personnel department won group approval. This inexpensive, highly satisfactory idea consisted of installing full-length mirrors in the waiting area adjacent to the elevators. The real cause for the complaints, reasoned the assistant, stemmed from the boring wait for the elevators, rather than from actual excessive waiting time. The mirrors were found to pleasantly distract the awaiting passengers, who could then glance at themselves and one another as they casually whiled away the few extra seconds required for the elevator to arrive. The moral of the fable is: "With reflection it becomes ap-

parent that there is more than one way to look at a problem."[12]

Devices such as brain-storming release creativity often
penned up by self-imposed constraints. If technical personnel
always assume that the causes and solutions of problems
are technical in nature, then a large spectrum of solutions—
including behavioral ones—are permanently eliminated.

Decision Making: Facts and Opinions

Step-by-step decision making tends to be fact-oriented. It
offers a structure for assessing problems and making decisions
founded on decision makers' perceptions of the facts. This
technique calls for reports and studies that offer necessary
back-up data and detail. This decision-making process is
logical, rational, and well documented. Once the process is
completed, it is assumed that, based on available information
and data, the "best" decision has been made. Such fact-
oriented decision making also calls for follow-through to
bolster implementation; making decisions is only part of a
larger overall managerial process.

Problems with fact-based decisions originate in inadequate *criteria of relevance*. The decision maker may hold
assumptions based on cultural or personal biases that clash
with the fundamental criteria used by those who are even-
tually charged with implementing the decision. According
to Drucker, "Most books on decision making tell the reader:
'First find the facts.' But managers who make effective decisions know that one does not start with facts. One starts
with opinions."[13]

Systematic consensus approaches, such as creative brain-
storming or the Japanese consensus procedure, lean toward
decisions that reflect collective opinions. The challenge in
this decision-making mode is to conciliate the participants'
opinions, which are essentially the ideas or judgments each
participant holds to be true. Each individual perceives the
facts through a reference frame and then negotiates differing

views until agreement is reached. Each person's opinion is tested throughout these proceedings and, in the final analysis, the collective level of information for making the decision is raised.

If those who carry out the decisions are included in the decision-making process, many of the implementation barriers characteristic of fact-based decision making are swept aside. The participants are committed to the project and will subsequently find a way to carry their part of the load.

Final Reminders

Two decision-making points call for special attention. First, in defining a problem and its causes, the search should be opened to unconventional solutions. A human-side solution, such as the mirrors in the elevator waiting area, may be appropriate and inexpensive when compared with a more technical approach. Perceiving the elevator problem from the human side as "boredom while waiting," as opposed to the engineering view of "inadequate passenger-moving capacity," opened the door to the simple solution adopted.

The second behavioral beacon shines a reminder that the process used in decision making deeply affects the implementation stage. When an individual or small group makes purely "fact-oriented" decisions, barriers to implementation are inevitably raised. Techniques such as the potential problem analysis become appropriate in such cases, to help manage the difficulties that are bound to appear. If, however, participative opinion-based decision making takes place, fewer behavioral roadblocks will appear during implementation. The extra effort and time necessary to reach a general consensus smooth the way for "easy behavioral sailing" during implementation of the decision.

References

1. Russell L. Ackoff, *The Art of Problem Solving* (New York: John Wiley & Sons, 1978), pp. 11–12.

2. *Ibid.*, pp. 11–12.
3. *Ibid.*, pp. 9, 77, 196–197.
4. John R. Thatcher, "The Rational Project Manager," *Project Management Institute Proceedings* (Boston, 1981), p. 231.
5. Adapted from C. H. Kepner and B. B. Tregoe, *The Rational Manager* (Princeton, N.J.: Kepner-Tregoe Inc., 1965), pp. 44–46.
6. *Ibid.*, pp. 48–50.
7. *Ibid.*, pp. 214–227.
8. Peter F. Drucker, *Management Tasks, Responsibilities, Practices* (New York: Harper & Row, 1974), p. 465.
9. William Ouchi, *Theory Z* (Reading, Mass.: Addison-Wesley, 1981), p. 43.
10. *Ibid.*, pp. 4–8.
11. *Ibid.*, p. 93.
12. Ackoff, *Problem Solving*, pp. 53–54.
13. Drucker, *Management Tasks*, pp. 470–471.

Chapter 13

Managing Change Across Changing Frontiers

"My dear, we live in a time of transition."
Adam, as he led Eve out of Paradise

The World Is Changing

As he left the comfort of the Garden of Eden and trudged into the unknown, Adam must have been the first person to comment on the changing times. Since then, the only thing that hasn't changed is change itself. In fact, the pace of change has accelerated in recent years as unprecedented advances in technology have been made. The environment has undergone immense, much heralded alterations. And the world economy continues to react to the constantly shifting powers of supply and demand. Concern about sources of energy generates interest in alternative as well as traditional supplies. Political attempts are made to juggle opposing forces into stable social structures.

All such changes have a profound impact on capital projects and, consequently, on project management. Project management, in fact, might be seen as a tool for managing change. Here is what prominent leaders who are directly and indirectly connected with project management have had to say about the occasionally scary, always fascinating changes that affect how projects are managed.

♦ *Technology.* Chris Kraft, upon retiring from the National Aeronautics and Space Administration, speculated about developments that may occur over the next several decades. He visualizes fully operational outer-space industries that are able to take advantage of zero-gravity conditions, in which materials of different densities do not separate and substances of different temperatures do not mix. He foresees a revolution in technology set off by increasing demand for communications devices, including digital mail, digital newspapers, and real-time information systems that interface with private companies and government agencies.[1]

♦ *Environment.* Margaret Mead put it bluntly: "We won't have a society if we destroy the environment."[2] Henry F. Le Mieux, while chairman of Raymond International, expressed similar concern, "Waste has become a serious problem, and clean water, clean air, and clean earth have become concerns. Our earth's resources, which both provide and absorb, are finite, so we must conserve our use of these resources. We must use them better and stabilize their rate of consumption. And above all, we must aggressively pursue alternatives."[3]

♦ *Economy.* The world's shifting economy shows little regard for individual desires—even those voiced by world leaders. As Nikita Khrushchev said, "Economics is a subject that does not greatly respect one's wishes."[4] National economies react faithfully to natural laws and forces that determine their behavior and often ultimately neglect the weaker segments of society. The challenges of inflation, economic growth, the trade imbalance, geopolitical instability, and petroleum price fluctuations place new demands on project environments.

♦ *Energy.* J. Robert Fluor, while president and chairman of Fluor Company, singled out the energy problem as "central to the economic well-being and national security of all industrialized nations. Beyond that, it also has a profound effect on the world's developing nations."[5]

♦ *Politics*. Politics is both the cause and the effect of transitional forces exerted by specific areas of interest. As the world continues to change, participation in the political process becomes ever more imperative.

Within this changing world, affected by technology, the environment, economics, energy, and politics, are a multitude of diverse projects. Some have been completed, others are under way, and some are still on the drawing board. Shifting economic, technological, and political conditions affect the feasibility of projects of all kinds. At one moment, all indicators may say go; the next moment, fluctuations in the external environment may kill projects on the drawing board, slow down ongoing project work, or cause a cutback in production of a completed project.

Such factors are beyond the control of project teams, which must accommodate overriding entrepreneurial and business concerns as major trends shift. If upper management decides to slow down or reduce a project significantly, the project team responsible for completing the project within quality, time, and cost parameters must adjust to meet the redefined goals. Such major trends are labeled "external environmental influences"; from the project team's standpoint, they remain fundamentally uncontrollable.

Trends and Project Management

How do project management professionals cope with change? First, by identifying trends, and second, by being on the leading edge of change as it evolves. Changes in technology, environment, national economies, and world politics all have uncontrollable influences on project management. Nevertheless, tendencies *can* be spotted, assumptions can be drawn, and educated guesses can be made regarding the possible impact on project management over time. The following trends will continue to have an ongoing effect on project management activities:

+ *Primary project technology.* Specialized project technologies such as those involving chemicals and pharmaceuticals will become even more sophisticated, thus placing stronger emphasis than ever on the management/specialist interface.
+ *Communications technology.* New forms of communciation will continue to move managerial working habits away from handling paper. More video, word processing, and voice techniques will be used.
+ *Project management technology.* New versions of scheduling and control systems will appear; however, project management tools will continue to be limited by human operational capacity and behavior. Systems will continue to be under-optimized.
+ *Size and nature of projects.* As economies slump, megaprojects will lose their appeal. Smaller ventures, including "refurbishing" jobs, will take on new dimensions. As economies recover, the trend will be to return to somewhat larger projects. As the world continues to "shrink," more ventures will be undertaken across cultural lines.
+ *Organizational behavior.* Increased emphasis will be given to behavior management as a fundamental support for project teams. New programs and training approaches will appear. Organizational structures will become increasingly amorphous, yet greater awareness of behavior management will allow people to work together with increased effectiveness.

Cross-Cultural Project Management

What is it about the international arena that keeps experienced project managers and tested, tried-and-true systems operating below par? Is it the language? The water? Different

weights and measures? Lack of local infrastructure? Or perhaps some sort of lingering "jet lag" that settles in for the
project's duration?

While notable success stories exist, a chat with conti-
nent-hopping project managers demonstrates that the school
of international hard knocks is alive and well—and living
in locales as diverse and exotic as Paris, New York, Djakarta,
and Rio de Janeiro. At international project symposia, "war
stories" roll off the tongues of scarred veterans as they
exchange thoughts and examine professional papers in search
of ways to improve performance. Problems with international
ventures range from tolerable differences in cultural traits
to entrenched antagonism culminating in major crises.

International projects offer a cozy nest where project
problems can roost. Verbal communication is thwarted when
people do not understand each other's languages. Procurement practices and ethics vary, logistics are unusually complex, and local foods don't please the foreign palate. Yet
such differences are often perfectly manageable. Measures
can be taken to move international obstacles aside and allow
projects to move ahead on course.

Traditions, language, experience, background, outlooks,
reasoning patterns, morals, and standards vary sharply from
one culture to another. Obvious differences may be confusing, such as the Bulgarian custom of nodding the head to
denote disapproval and shaking the head as a sign of ap-
probation. Or the variations may be more subtle. For instance, to an American, orange is a bright color describing
the hue of a fruit bearing the same name; to a Brazilian,
the same color is simply known as "a darker shade of
yellow."

Differences in the way people see things can lead to
minuscule distortions in daily routines, which, if allowed to
snowball, can create major deviations in project results. The
things that are different on projects are manageable. Differences in people, however, are more difficult to handle, and
it's those "people differences" that often constitute the chief
cause of problems on international projects.

On domestic, or "all-in-one-country," projects, cultural disparities among organizations, subgroups, and individuals have a signficant impact. In the international arena, where the potential problems are substantially magnified, cultural gaps must be bridged. One or both sides must reach over to help establish a common base of communication. On domestic projects, developing cross-cultural thinking among organizations or groups is a challenging yet attainable goal, because the individuals involved tend to have language, nationality, and working habits in common. On international projects, however, bridging the cultural gap may be a project in itself.

Culture and Management Style

By culture, we mean those underlying philosophies that influence how people go about doing things and how they expect others to perform and react. In the context of behavior patterns in organizations, culture constitutes the shared ideas and beliefs that are associated with a way of life in an organization. Based on case studies, attempts have been made to classify distinct types of organizational culture. Hay Associates identified the following three culturally distinct styles:

+ *Bureaucratic:* existing in many French and Japanese companies
+ *Technological:* typical of businesses in Germany and Great Britain, particularly companies in traditional industries, where the style is paternalistic
+ *Management:* native to the Netherlands and Switzerland, also embraced by most U.S. firms, where the manager is a leader and a team player[6]

Intercultural Understanding

When cultures are mixed, however, the path to understanding is strewn with obstacles. "Mixing" cultures may involve bringing together people from different countries or intermingling personnel from organizations that have dif-

ferent managerial philosophies. Three qualities are required
to achieve mutual or intercultural understanding:

1. Commonality to ensure some shared grounds as a
   basis for overall agreement
2. Differentiality to add dimension and the opportunity
   to learn
3. Flexibility to ensure interaction and offer growth[7]

Intercultural differences are sparks that can touch off
major conflicts. Potential problems in mixed settings are
often not anticipated because cultural assumptions are not
considered. Cultural conflict occurs over apparently simple
things, like time, for instance. In some countries promptness
is expected as a matter of course; tardiness is reproved and
can become a source of irritation. In other cultures, ap-
pointments are made within a general time frame and not
at a specific hour. When individuals from these differing
cultures interact, conflict is likely. People with time-conscious backgrounds feel insulted at having to wait past an
appointed hour. Individuals used to a loose time frame are
equally upset by the lack of comprehension on the part of
overly time-conscious visitors. They react with views like,
"He should understand that other pressing matters came up
that had to be dealt with so that I could later give him my
undivided attention."

Such gaps can only be closed by intercultural understanding—when both parties have an awareness of what
makes others act as they do and recognize that the source
of misunderstanding is the culture, not the person.

Project managers and others working in the international
environment must be on the lookout for two fundamental
cultural barriers. The first is the tendency to use self-ref-
erence criteria, in which everything is judged according to
the seer's own values. Culture shock, the bewildering impact
that results from strange customs and ways, is the second
barrier to be hurdled. Since getting the job done is more
important than doing it "your" way, cultural alternatives
should be taken into account before habit-based decisions

are made. Respect for alternative ways of doing things may cut down on conflict and increase project performance. Different avenues must be objectively considered to stave off potential problems in intercultural understanding.

Cross-Cultural Organizations

Organizations are designed to help people interact effectively to accomplish tasks. If the organization is set within a consistent cultural context, the structure will reflect a predominant philosophy, be it bureaucratic, technical, or managerial in nature. If, however, cultures are mixed, the organization must be adapted to cross-cultural needs.

A case history involving facilities for the written press at the 1976 Olympic Games in Montreal illustrates the point. In spite of an acknowledged need to centralize management of the press-center facilities—which required planning the physical layout and equipment tie-ins, installing and arranging telecommunications and switching gear, and training operating personnel—strong political and social opposition blocked the appointment of an overall project manager. It was feared that the project manager would be a powerful authority figure. The solution was to appoint a communications coordinator who reported to a management steering committee. That person coordinated the activities of the associated organizations, which in turn were directed by their own individual project managers. This solution, which proved effective, although unconventional, was a result of cross-cultural sensitivity.[8]

A more typical cross-cultural organization is the joint venture, which is common in engineering and construction circles. Rarely do the organizational cultures of joint venture partners coincide; therefore, the new structure must accommodate significant differences. Sometimes this is done by partially duplicating certain positions or splitting the main functions, so that each partner operates by its own rules within assigned spheres of responsibility.

Development programs in Third World countries represent another cross-cultural situation. Individual projects

operating under the umbrella of a major development program are subject to the cultural influence of the entity that
administers the program. A special group may have to be
created within the project to deal interculturally with such
government agencies or financing entities.

From a structural standpoint, cross-cultural action takes
place when abrupt changes come about in organizational
philosophy—for instance, when personnel accustomed to
operating laterally across authority lines find themselves
working within a vertical organization.

Project management imposes a horizontal dimension on
the traditional vertical organization; as a result, many people
have come to think of project management as "horizontal
management." In some organizations, they say, project ideas
are so well ingrained that a horizontal culture appears to
exist. Regardless of the organization's original nature, when
the structure is shifted, organizational culture shock may
appear unless swift strides are taken to reach a cross-cultural
understanding.

Technology Transfer

New technologies developed in the industrialized world are
"imported" by developing nations. How well that importation
process works determines to a great extent whether the
technology stays behind after a project is completed, or if
it returns to the homeland in the memories and briefcases
of repatriated project technicians. Technology is not transferred, for example, when so-called "black box" deals are
made. In this case, the new plant or facility stays in-country,
but the design and implementation know-how remains only
as long as the supplier's technicians are present. The "black
box" plant does what it's supposed to do, but its technology
remains a mystery to the new owners.

In Latin America, technology transfer has become the
target for special studies and legislation aimed at protecting

the receiving country's interests. Objectives common to most Latin American technology transfer policies are:

♦ The need to conserve foreign exchange
♦ The desire to increase the level of industrialization
♦ The desire to obtain better commercial deals that will ensure that the recipient is not left "holding the bag"

Technology transfer policies are generally applicable to all Third World development needs. Independent local capability is a goal for most countries that are striving to improve their technical infrastructure.

Whether technology is transferred through trade, direct foreign investment, or licensing agreements, there is growing desire among developing countries for more cogent and effective technology transfer. To attain this goal, transfer requirements must be built into contractual agreements, otherwise vendors may have no interest in opening up their "black boxes." It may be, after all, to the vendors' advantage to keep the mysterious boxes as "black" as possible in order to shore up technical service backlogs and stimulate sales of related goods and services. Developing countries, however, are increasingly insistent in requiring a reasonable extent of technical transfer even for highly sophisticated technologies.

Conveying technology ushers a new factor into project work, and it may add a twist to the task of actually managing the project. The extent to which project management is affected depends on whether the technology is shifted between two developed nations or from an industrialized to a developing country. Developed countries usually have experienced people available who can become familiar with a new technology through conventional orientation programs and practical training. For developing countries, however, this is not always the case. Hamed K. Eldin says that the receiving developing country "usually will have a critical shortage of experienced people in most technical areas."[9] This means extensive educational and training efforts are needed to pass along the technology.

Transferring technology from an industrialized nation to a developing country requires that more people be involved in the project implementation phase. Not only must the project be organized, structured, managed, and directed to meet normal project requirements, but a continuous on-the-job training program must be conducted throughout implementation.

Key project personnel may thus find themselves blessed with permanent "shadows" from the sponsoring nation's operation, who steadfastly dog their steps in order to "capture" as much technology as possible. While this obviously enchances transfer of the technology, it can be troublesome for those managing the project: interference, explanations, adjustments, and changes are bound to occur. Because the host country's engineers and other specialists often have experience in similar technologies or related fields and are usually well educated, they naturally generate ideas and wish to make significant contributions. These suggestions require discussion and consideration, involving once again the time and patience of the people who are supposed to be accomplishing the basic project work. This involvement can set the stage for conflict. Nicholas Chryssafopoulos, a partner of Dames & Morse, stated in a trade magazine commentary: "Often, whether justified or not, the recipient's nationalism and distrust of everything foreign translates into an attitude of 'I know all there is to know, I don't need you,' and the wheel keeps on being reinvented."[10]

For project management, technology transfer means an additional variable to juggle—one more activity that must be diplomatically managed throughout the project. The topic thus requires serious interface planning and evaluation in order to bridge the political and cultural gaps between the "transferer" and the "transferee."

Conclusion

In a world of transition where dramatic technological changes are commonplace and substantial fluctuations in capital investment can occur at a moment's notice, project management personnel are faced with increasingly exacting demands. The skyrocketing number of cross-cultural projects and the new project influences such as technology transfer add to the burden. How can project teams cope with the accelerating rate of complexity?

People can always solve their own problems—particularly in project management, because problem solving is what project management is all about. By drawing on the tools of the trade, such as planning, interfacing, training, negotiating, and decision making, project managers can overcome even the most awesome barriers. Although the project arena is complex, with many factors becoming uncontrollable, management tools *can* be honed to meet the challenges as they appear, especially when managers are attuned to the human side of project management.

References

1. Rosanne Clark, "Chris Kraft: NASA's Teacher Steps Down," *Houston Magazine* (September 1982), p. 22.
2. Laurence J. Peter, *Peter's Quotations* (New York: William Morrow, 1973), p. 20.
3. Henry F. Le Mieux, "The '80s—Dangers and Opportunities," in *The Dangerous Decade—A Forecast of Some Challenging Opportunities for Project Management*, John R. Adams and Nicki S. Kirchof, eds. (Drexel Hill, Pa: Project Management Institute, 1981), pp. 14–15.
4. Cited in Peter, *Peter's Quotations*, p. 470.
5. J. Robert Fluor, "The 1980s: A Decade for Trends and Changes," in *The Dangerous Decade—A Forecast of Some Challenging Opportunities for Project Management*, John R. Adams and Nicki S. Kirchof, eds. (Drexel Hill, Pa: Project Management Institute, 1981), p. 24.

6. D. George Harris, "How National Cultures Shape Management Styles," *Management Review*, vol. 71, no. 7 (July 1982), p. 58.
7. Pierre Casse, "The Cross-Cultural Mind," *The Bridge* (Spring 1980), p. 7.
8. Robert B. Gills, "The 'Communication Coordinator'—An Experimental Approach to Project Control," *Project Management Institute Proceedings* (Chicago, October 1977), p. 143.
9. Russell D. Archibald, "Technology Transfer in Cross Boundary Projects," *Managing International Projects* (Zurich: Gottlieb Duttweiler Institute, November–December 1977), p. 102.
10. Nicholas Chryssafopoulos, "Meaning What We Say About Technology Transfer," *Worldwide Projects Magazine* (July 1982), pp. 1–2.

Chapter 14

Human Behavior as Seen by the Experts

Few of us understand why we behave as we do, but we are convinced that we have such understanding.

Russell L. Ackoff and James R. Emshoff

Theories of human behavior are plentiful. Over the years, philosophers, psychiatrists, psychologists, professors, practitioners, and lay persons have all expressed their views on the subject. Some of their opinions have been grouped into managerial behavioral theories, which provide explanations for human behavior when people are organized in a structural form to achieve established goals. Because a project's success is strongly dependent on effectively managing human behavior, selected theories of behavior are presented here as a reference for the behavioral discussions presented in the previous chapters.

Internal vs. External Causation

The ancient Greeks argued about whether behavior was determined by "inherent characteristics" or by "environmental influences." Volumes of scholarly works supporting one or the other school grace the shelves of libraries around the world. And the nature-nurture debate over the origin of human behavior continues today.

Internal causes of behavior are largely of a cognitive mental nature, derived from the individual's own process of perception. External causation refers to environmental influences on behavior. In *Behavior Management*, Lawrence M. Miller points out a philosophical difference between the thoughts of Plato and Aristotle. Plato believed that behavior resulted from how people were taught by their educators and their social system. He set out, therefore, to establish the "Republic," the ideal social system designed to optimize learning. Aristotle believed that human behavior was a result of the instinctive and unchanging inherent nature of man. Says Miller, "These two views of the determinants of behavior, while somewhat modified and certainly decorated with dozens of supplemental theories, remain the essential distinctions between current theories of psychology."[1]

The project manager's search for the answer to what makes people act and react must begin at the very foundations of behavioral theory, set forth thousands of years ago by Plato and Aristotle. Management behavior and motivation theories that emphasize the interface between internal and external causation are popular among managers and organizational training specialists. According to Miller, motivation theories are based on the perception of interaction between individuals and the external environment, yet such interaction is considered to take place in the internal motivation state. Motivation theories assert that "somewhere between the occurrence of an event or circumstance in the environment and the behavior, there is arousal or change in a state of motivation. This state is presumably within the individual."[2]

Changes in Behavior

As leader of the panel discussion on behavior at the Fourteenth Project Management Institute Symposium held in

Toronto, Michael McCaskey asked panel members, "Do you think you are able to teach behavior change to project managers?"

Panelist Robert Youker of the World Bank responded candidly, "I think the evidence is clear that by the time someone is four or five years old, their basic personality profile is well settled, and that you don't make major changes in people's personalities. You can make marginal changes or you may influence their environment."[3] Behavioral experts tend to support that view. Some psychologists claim that few personality changes can be made after the early formative years, which may extend until age seven or eight.

On the other hand, there are those who insist that substantial changes in behavior can occur even after early formative years. The concept that behavior can be changed through dedicated and persistent effort is sometimes known as the "Pygmalion Effect." According to Greek mythology, Pygmalion was an artist whose sculptured statue of a beautiful woman subsequently came to life. As stated by J. Sterling Livingston, ". . . In the world of management, many executives play Pygmalion-like roles in developing able subordinates and in stimulating their performance."[4]

Livingston implies that a manager's expectations are a strong factor in causing behavioral change: "If a manager's expectations are high, productivity is likely to be excellent. If his expectations are low, productivity is likely to be poor."[5]

Any type of behavioral change is generally accomplished through a methodical process that is both time-consuming and arduous. Changes in behavior can occur in one of four levels or areas: (1) knowledge, (2) attitude, (3) individual behavior, or (4) group behavior.[6] Changes in knowledge are the fastest and easiest to process. At the other extreme, altering group behavior is a drawn-out, tedious undertaking. Changes in individual attitudes and behavior represent intermediate states of difficulty and time duration.

Behavioral change—even in adults—can be brought about, yet the journey may be long and tiring. Persistence, patience, and self-discipline are key factors in inducing such change.

People Are Alike—People Are Different

In supporting the position that people are basically alike, Harold J. Leavitt proposes a system in which needs, wants, tensions, or discomforts are provoked by a stimulus (or cause) that is designed to meet or attenuate those needs, wants, tensions, or discomforts.[7] Each change is fed back into the system, which adjusts itself to the new stimulus that resulted from achieving or not achieving the goal.

In this basic model, behavior is seen as an effort to eliminate tensions by achieving goals that remove the causes of tensions. In asserting that people are all basically the same, Leavitt relates three assumptions about human behavior: "(1) Behavior is caused, (2) behavior is motivated, (3) behavior is goal-directed."[8] These assumptions form a feedback loop. The cause stimulates the motive, which in turn is directed toward the goal.

The view that each person is unique is an outgrowth of a newer philosophy of individuality. In support of that view, Leavitt points out that people are born with certain physical needs; later, social, egoistic, or psychological needs are acquired or emerge. Psychological needs stem not only from physical needs but also from the nervous system of the physical body itself and from a natural dependence on other people.

Hierarchy of Human Needs

According to Abraham Maslow: "There are at least five sets of goals which we may call basic needs. These are briefly, physiological, safety, love, esteem, and self-actualization. These basic goals are related to one another, being arranged in a hierarchy of prepotency."[9] Maslow's theory refers to various states of deprivation and points out that, given such states, human behavior will be appreciably affected. For instance, when faced with the choice between the need for food and the desire for self-actualization, the need for food will predominate. Likewise, following Maslow's theory, the need for love will predominate over that for esteem.

The needs-hierarchy theory, while representing an orderly academic arrangement of concepts, may seem irrelevant to many managers. As Miller comments, "How many industrial supervisors, when instructed in Maslow's hierarchy of needs, have reacted with a silent 'so what?' What is the supervisor supposed to do with this information? Provide food, safety, love, esteem, or self-actualization to his employees?"[10] The theory may be seen as excessively simplistic and of little practical application. However, the value of Maslow's work may not be in the theory itself but in the groundwork it lays for other motivational researchers, such as Frederick Herzberg and Douglas McGregor.

The Motivation-Hygiene Theory

"Job satisfaction versus job dissatisfaction" is the theme of Frederick Herzberg's motivation-hygiene theory. He developed the theory in an attempt to relate Maslow's hierarchy to on-the-job situations. The research arena was Pittsburgh, where 200 engineers and accountants from 11 industries were interviewed.[11] The data led Herzberg to conclude that there are two distinct types of needs relating to the work situation which are independent of one another and affect behavior in different ways.

Factors associated with job dissatisfaction tended to relate to the environment or surroundings. These dissatisfiers Herzberg calls *hygiene* or *maintenance* factors, because of their preventive and environmental nature. The results of Herzberg's study imply that workers tend not to be unsatisfied if certain hygiene or maintenance factors are kept within acceptable standards.

Herzberg relates hygiene factors to basic physiological needs, safety, and love, and believes that certain "lower" needs must first be taken care of on a maintenance basis in order to avoid job dissatisfaction.

To create job satisfaction or motivation, another set of variables comes into play. The survey indicated that job satisfiers were related to the *work*, not the surroundings. These items Herzberg calls *motivators*, because they potentially elevate workers to superior levels of performance. The motivation factors correspond to the higher end of Maslow's scale, which includes esteem and self-actualization.

Herzberg's fundamental message is that eliminating dissatisfaction is not sufficient for creating satisfaction. Achievement, recognition, challenges, increasing responsibility, and opportunities for growth and development are necessary job satisfiers or motivators.

Theory X and Theory Y

Douglas McGregor's classic "Theory X–Theory Y" sheds light on managers' dealings with their subordinates. Theory X assumes that most people prefer to be directed, that they are not interested in taking on responsibilities, and that they are basically looking for security. Theory X also assumes that people are largely motivated by money, position, and punishment. Under Theory X, it is assumed that (1) work is a disagreeable task—something that people prefer to avoid and from which they derive no enjoyment, (2) people have little capacity for creativity and problem solving, and (3) motivation occurs at Maslow's levels of physiological and security needs. Managers who subscribe to Theory X tend to impose tight organizational structures and strict supervisory controls. They believe that such an arrangement is necessary because workers are immature and lack a sense of responsibility.

In analyzing the Theory X assumptions, McGregor questioned their validity and proposed an alternative view of human behavior called Theory Y. This approach assumes that people are not inherently lazy, that they tend to meet positive expectations if appropriately motivated. It postulates that people can direct themselves to be both creative and responsible in work, provided their human potential as workers is stimulated. Theory Y assumes that work is a natural function—as natural as playing a game, for instance. Employee self-discipline is part of human nature and is required to meet organizational goals. Creativity and problem-solving functions should be distributed throughout the organization. Motivation occurs at Maslow's higher levels of esteem and self-actualization.[12]

Those managers who subscribe to Theory Y tend to establish less structured organizations and exert limited control and supervision over the work force. Such managers emphasize employee development and growth and encourage subordinates to become increasingly independent in performing tasks within the company's best interests. McGregor's conclusions imply that the Theory Y approach is the more desirable managerial philosophy to follow.[13]

No one theory can adequately capture the subtleties of behavior management, but each concept provides a foundation for testing and projecting other views. In their article "Beyond Theory Y," John J. Morse and Jay W. Lorsch present their "contingency theory."[14] They expand on the idea that appropriate organizational patterns are contingent on the nature of the work and on the needs of the people involved.

Theory Z

Theory Z, while not an extension of Theory X–Theory Y, can be related to McGregor's concepts. In *Theory Z*, William Ouchi describes Western "Type Z" companies, which share some characteristics with Japanese organizations. For instance, the Z company tends toward long-term employment, with employees working in various functions and posts during different periods of their careers. Z organizations are well-versed in formal planning, control, and management information systems, but the data generated by such mechanisms is carefully weighed against subjective criteria involving organizational "fit" and suitability.[15]

In a Z company it is assumed that people are responsible
and are capable of achieving excellence when they are
motivated by appeals to their social well-being, self-esteem,
and self-actualization. An illustration of that point is Ouchi's
reference to egalitarianism as a central feature of Type Z
organizations. Egalitarianism means that people can be trusted
and can work autonomously without close supervision. According to Ouchi, "This feature, perhaps more than any
other, accounts for the high levels of commitment, loyalty,
and productivity in Japanese firms and in Type Z organizations."[16]

Expectancy Theory

If there is an expectation for favorable change, then motivation will take place. This explanation for the causes of
motivation and the subsequent influences on individual behavior is called the "expectancy theory." It is based on the
concept that people choose behaviors that they believe will
lead to a desired outcome.

The expectancy theory offers an explanation about how
people choose among alternative behaviors. It focuses on
individuals rather than on groups. The theory is cognitive
in nature and constitutes an internal approach to motivation
and behavioral causation.[17] The theory contends that individuals assess the probability of achieving certain goals by
identifying the following:

- *Effort-to-performance expectancy.* This represents the
  individual's perception of the probability of meeting
  goals and the difficulty of attaining the required level
  of performance.
- *Performance-to-outcome expectancy.* This is the individual's perception of the probability of achieving a
  certain outcome, given the performance level required.

♦ *Valence.* Valence is the value the individual places on the outcome.

Thus, Branch suggests that individuals faced with alternatives ask themselves: "Can I do the job expected of me?" (effort-to-performance expectancy), "If I do the job, what will be the consequences for me?" (performance-to-outcome expectancy), and "Is it really worth the effort required of me?" (valence). Individuals thus search out their own personal justification for becoming motivated.[18]

Transactional Analysis (TA)

Transactional Analysis (TA) postulates that all people have, in differing degrees, three ego states—child, parent, and adult. Eric Berne points out, however, that "although we cannot directly observe these ego states, we can observe behavior and from this infer which of the three ego states is operating at that moment."[19]

Natural impulses learned from childhood experiences are associated with the child ego state, corresponding to reactions induced by a purely emotional base. The parent ego state results from the influences of parents, teachers, and other powerful figures in early childhood. Rational behavior, on the other hand, is the product of the adult ego state. People are thus governed by three conflicting yet complementary factors: (1) the emotional content of the child, (2) the values carried by the parent, and (3) the rationality of the adult ego state. Healthy people maintain a balance among all three ego states, even though everyone operates in the states at different times.

Another well-known postulate of TA is the "I'm OK, you're OK" slogan, which proposes that basic attitudes mold people's personalities. These are life positions that vary from "I'm not OK, you're not OK," through the interim positions of "I'm OK, you're not OK" and "I'm not OK, you're OK," to "I'm OK, you're OK." TA suggests that depending on their life positions, people need to be "stroked" and recognized as individuals, thus inferring a need for reassurance regarding personal worth and competence.

Situational Leadership

In the situational leadership theory developed by Hersey and Blanchard, four leadership styles are identified: "telling," "selling," "participating," and "delegating."[20] Each of the four styles represents a combination of *task behavior* (the extent to which a leader provides direction for people) and *relationship behavior* (the extent to which a leader engages in two-way communication with people). Which style is appropriate depends on the maturity level of the people being supervised. Maturity levels occur across a continuum labeled as follows:

M1	Low maturity
M2	Low to moderate maturity
M3	Moderate to high maturity
M4	High maturity

For directing low maturity (M1) people who are both unable and unwilling to take on responsibility, "telling" is the prescribed leadership style. The leader should take a directive approach, spelling out instructions clearly and specifically. Low-to-moderate (M2) maturity levels are best dealt with by using a "selling" leadership style. An M2 audience is "unable but willing" to take responsibility, thus a selling stance provides both directive and supportive behaviors to raise the ability level. For M3 groups, which are able but unwilling to cooperate, the "participating" approach is appropriate. The leader should assume a supportive, nondirective role in relating to people of moderate-to-high maturity level. At high maturity levels (M4), leaders are able to take on a "delegating" posture. The audience is both willing and able to assume responsibility. Little direction or support is necessary because mature individuals are capable of carrying out work with limited task or behavioral support.

The Dimensional Model of Managerial Behavior

The dimensional model of managerial behavior developed by Lefton *et al.* presents four aspects of managerial styles: (1) dominance, (2) submission, (3) hostility, and (4) warmth.[21] The hostility-warmth continuum is depicted along a horizontal axis, while the dominance-submission continuum is presented along a vertical axis. Thus, a matrix is formed that contains the following quadrants:

Dominance-hostility.	Represents "tell-and-do management"
Hostility-submission.	Characterizes "don't-rock-the-boat management"
Warmth-submission.	A "let's be pals" management style
Dominance-warmth.	"Benefit-optimizing management"

According to the dimensional model, a manager's style essentially falls into one which describes the manager's primary strategy. The manager's daily behavior, however, varies considerably according to the situation, the subordinate's experience level and self-confidence, each person's assessment of what is at stake, and economic factors. Individual managers, subordinates, and supervisors have different characteristics; therefore, each interpersonal relationship is unique. Managers must custom tailor their approach in dealing with each individual.

The Managerial Grid®

An often-cited concept and popular training theme for identifying managerial traits is Blake and Mouton's Managerial

Grid®, a matrix that is used to indicate the relationship between two concerns: (1) people (subordinates and colleagues) and (2) production (work results). These concerns, plotted on rectilinear coordinate axes, highlight differing management styles by pinpointing how managers interrelate the two. The horizontal axis displays the manager's concern for production, while the vertical axis indicates the manager's concern for people. The resulting Grid permits a graphic display of management styles, ranging from the authoritarian leader who is unconcerned with people to the "nice person" who is so wrapped up with people that production is neglected.

The axes of the Grid are scaled from 1 to 9, as shown in Figure 14-1. Blake and Mouton identified five leadership styles, which are uniquely positioned on the Grid. Each style is indicated and described in Figure 14-1.

Other Behavior Studies

Other studies and theories considered significant in the specialized literature related to organizational behavior are summarized below.[22]

Achievement Motivation

According to David C. McClelland and his associates, achievement-oriented people have certain characteristics in common. They prefer to establish their own goals and don't respond well unless they are involved in doing so. They tend to set difficult but achievable goals—targets that can be reached but will represent a challenge. Personal achievement is more important than the rewards of success. They are more interested in task-related feedback than behavioral feedback. In other words, they prefer to know how their job is coming along rather than how they are being perceived by others.

Figure 14–1. The Managerial Grid ®.

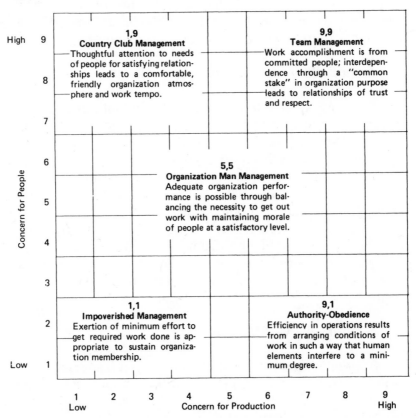

Source: Robert R. Blake and Jane S. Mouton, *The New Managerial Grid*® (Houston: Gulf Publishing, 1978), p. 11. Reproduced by permission.

Activities, Interactions, and Sentiments

Certain activities, interactions, and sentiments are required for a group to perform its tasks. This model, developed by George C. Homans of the "interactionist" school, assumes that activities requiring personal interactions are performed. As people interact, certain attitudes and sentiments are developed. If the sentiments are positive, new activities will develop among the members (they socialize, participate in bowling leagues, and so on). This leads to the development of norms that specify expectations for behavior in certain situations. When negative sentiments occur among group members, mutually supportive norms do not develop.

Immaturity-Maturity Theory

Chris Argyris contends that an individual's development proceeds along a continuum from immaturity to maturity as the person moves from childhood through mature adulthood. People move from a passive state to one of increasing activity; from dependence upon others to relative independence; from behaving in limited ways to behaving in many ways; from casual, sporadic, and shallow interests to more profound commitments; from a now-oriented time perspective to a broad-based one; from subordination to others to an equal or superior position in relation to others; and from a lack of self-awareness to awareness and a sense of self-control.

Leadership Continuum

Tannenbaum and Schmidt represented leadership styles along a continuum moving from authoritarian leadership at one end to democratic leadership at the other. Authoritarian leaders tend to tell subordinates what to do and how to do it, while democratic leaders tend to share responsibilities by involving subordinates in the planning and execution of tasks.

Leadership Contingency Model

According to Fred E. Fiedler, there is no "best" leadership style. Generalizations about effective styles do not necessarily apply for particular situations. Fiedler found three variables determining favorable or unfavorable situations for leaders: (1) leader-member relationships, (2) degree of task structure, and (3) position power. The leader's situations were found to range from "most favorable" (in which the leader is liked by the group, has power, and directs a well-defined job) to "least favorable" (in which the leader is disliked, has little position power, and is responsible for an unstructured task). In searching for a most effective leadership style, Fiedler found that task-oriented leaders are successful in situations that are considered either favorable or unfavorable to the leader, while relationship-oriented leaders are more successful in intermediate situations that are neither favorable nor unfavorable.

Differentiation and Integration Model

According to Lawrence and Lorsch, the design of an organization and its subsystems must fit the environment; therefore, there is no "right" way to design an organization. Two concepts are considered important in organizational design: differentiation and integration. Differentiation stresses the differences in management orientations and formal structure among different functional departments. Each department, therefore, is a subsystem in which members develop particular orientations and structural tasks. The state of collaboration is identified as integration and reflects the effort among departments to achieve unity.

Force-Field Analysis

Both driving and restraining forces influence tendencies toward change, according to Kurt Lewin. Driving forces affect situations that move in a particular direction; thus they tend to both initiate and maintain the tendency to change. Pressures from the home office, punitive supervision, and job security are examples of driving forces. Restraining forces act to attenuate such drives. Resentment, lack of coordination, and short-cutting the chain of command are examples of restraining forces. Organizational equilibrium occurs when the driving forces offset the restraining forces. The equilibrium is unstable and can be changed if the relative intensity of the driving or restraining force changes.

Human Behavior and Project Management

The behavior theories that have been summarized in this chapter are intended to apply to all organizational contexts—including project management. Yet most of the studies of management behavior are conducted in an industrial production context. However, some research has focused specifically on management behavior in project work. In his paper "Project Management and Behavioral Research Revisited," Stephen D. Owens reviewed studies performed in the behavioral area of project management. Owens synthesized findings from five key areas: (1) leadership behavior in the project group, (2) motivational techniques, (3) interpersonal and organizational communication, (4) conflict management, and (5) decision-making and team-building skills. Pertinent findings drawn from Owens' summary are given as follows:

- *Leadership behavior.* Project managers cannot rely on one particular leadership style to influence other people's behavior. Different situations call for different approaches, and leaders must be sensitive to the unique features of circumstances and personalities.
- *Motivational techniques.* An awareness of unfulfilled needs residing in the group is required to successfully appraise motivational requirements and adjust a job's design to meet those needs.
- *Interpersonal and organizational communication.* Conflict situations occur regularly. A problem-solving or confrontation approach, using informal group sessions, can be a useful resolution strategy.
- *Decision-making and team-building skills.* Participative decision making meets the needs of individual team members and contributes toward effective decisions and team unity.[23]

The findings of Baker and Wilemon, although less recent than those of Owens, are also significant. Baker and Wilemon arrived at the following general conclusions:

- In project management, there is no panacea that governs behavior management—each project situation is unique.
- Although the project manager should have as much authority as possible, he or she should operate through influence rather than through wielding formal authority.
- The problem-solving approach is the most successful mode for conflict resolution; participative decision making, which stimulates commitment, teamwork, and a sense of mission, is effective in project management.
- Higher degrees of "projectization" reduce the probability of cost and schedule overruns.
- Perceived success largely depends on effective coordination and relations patterns.[24]

Theory vs. Practice

Project people who have come up through the school of hard knocks tend to question theoretical insights into a project's problems. This remains true whether the theories are derived from general behavior studies or specific research on the human side of project management. Erwin S. Stanton comments on the reaction of seasoned managers to motivational concepts in his book *Reality-Centered People Management*: "The concepts might indeed sound very good in theory, but [managers'] own experiences have shown that in practice the principles simply do not always work well. In fact, at times, they do not work at all."[25] Managers are thus struck by the dramatic inconsistency between the academic simplicity of behavioral and motivational theories and the nuts-and-bolts reality of on-the-job project management.

Many experienced managers prefer a shirtsleeves approach that is based on their backgrounds. Resistance to theories is understandable—after all, managers generally reach their position of responsibility as a result of their past successes and inherent attributes. Many of them believe in the axiom: "If it works, don't fix it." Project managers who have had little or no training in behavior management techniques may reject what is unfamiliar to them.

In the theories, lines are firmly drawn between the camps of internal and external causation, Theory X and Theory Y, attitude and behavior change, and hygiene and motivational factors. Other needs or motivating factors are neatly tagged and assigned priorities (hierarchy of needs), while others are boxed into grid or matrix formats. As all project professionals know, the real world isn't that simple.

John D. Borcherding points out the danger of unquestioned allegiance to production-based behavioral theories in capital project applications: "In construction, the goal is to build a unique structure—one which has never been built before. In contrast, the industrial organization seeks to build repetitively a large number of identical products. These two facts alone give rise to a host of further diversionary characteristics."[26]

During day-to-day project work, behavioral shadings emerge that are not easy to categorize. For instance, people's differing perceptions about the importance of work, the need for autonomy versus participation, and the need for money can alter human behavior in many ways. And those "difficult" people can turn even the most objective project atmosphere into a touchy setting.

Behavioral theories rarely point firmly to a practical solution. Yet, based on surveys, studies, or deductive reasoning, they do provide a framework for observations on tendencies or groupings of certain behavioral characteristics. The resulting classifications of dominant characteristics may indeed be challenged by the question "In relation to what?" For instance, a manager may be aggressive toward subordinates, submissive to the boss, distant from the family, and playful with the dog. The same person exhibits different behavior depending on the position, context, and profile of the other figuring characters.

Even if theories about behavior can be questioned, they do offer insights into patterns. A theoretical background in organizational behavior might be considered analogous to one in music. Knowledge of music theory is not sufficient to make one a superb musician, but can augment natural talent and diligence. In some cases, however, talent and desire are sufficient to propel people to the top, as in the case of the acclaimed musician who can't decipher a note of music, or the eminently successful project manager who has never read an article on management behavior or participated in related training programs. Yet, for most people, a foundation in theory—whether in music or behavior management—can give a helpful boost toward sharpening perception, thus opening new doors for advancement and professional growth.

References

1. Lawrence M. Miller, *Behavior Management* (New York: John Wiley & Sons, 1978), p. 20.
2. *Ibid.*, p. 27.
3. Quoted from panel session led by Michael B. McCaskey, "Workshop on Teaching Project Management," Project Management Institute Symposium, Toronto, October 2–3, 1982.
4. J. Sterling Livingston, "Pygmalion in Management," *Harvard Business Review* (July–August 1969), p. 45.
5. *Ibid.*, p. 45.
6. Paul Hersey and Kenneth H. Blanchard, *Psicologia para Administradores de Empresas* (São Paulo, Brazil: Editora Pedagógica e Universitária Ltda., 1977), p. 2.
7. Harold J. Leavitt, *Managerial Psychology* (Chicago: University of Chicago Press, 1972), pp. 5–6.
8. *Ibid.*, p. 10.
9. Cited in Miller, *Behavior Management*, p. 27.
10. *Ibid.*, p. 29.
11. Frederick Herzberg, Bernard Mausner, and Barbara Snyderman, *The Motivation to Work* (New York: John Wiley & Sons, 1959), p. ix.

12. Hersey and Blanchard, *Psicologia*, pp. 59–62.
13. Douglas McGregor, *The Human Side of Enterprise* (New York: McGraw-Hill, 1960), p. 246.
14. John J. Morse and Jay W. Lorsch, "Beyond Theory Y," *Harvard Business Review*, Motivation Series No. 21137 (May–June 1970), pp. 37–44.
15. William Ouchi, *Theory Z—How American Business Can Meet the Japanese Challenge* (Philippines: Addison-Wesley, 1981).
16. *Ibid.*, p. 81.
17. Miller, *Behavior Management*, p. 39.
18. Kenneth J. Branch, "Motivation and Matrix Management," *Project Management Institute Proceedings* (Toronto, 1982), p. III-L.2.
19. Eric Berne, *Principles of Group Treatment* (New York: Oxford University Press, 1964), p. 281.
20. Paul Hersey and Kenneth H. Blanchard, *Management of Organizational Behavior* (Englewood Cliffs, N.J.: Prentice-Hall, 1982), pp. 149–173.
21. R. E. Lefton, V. R. Buzzotta, and Mannie Sherberg, *Dimensional Management Strategies* (St. Louis: Psychological Associates, 1978), pp. 6–11.
22. This section adapted from material presented in Robert H. Guest, Paul Hersey, and Kenneth H. Blanchard, *Organizational Change Through Effective Leadership* (Englewood Cliffs, N.J.: Prentice-Hall, 1977), pp. 57–73.
23. Stephen D. Owens, "Project Management and Behavioral Research Revisited," *Project Management Institute Proceedings* (Toronto, 1982), p. II-F.1.
24. Bruce N. Baker and David L. Wilemon, "A Summary of Major Research Findings Regarding the Human Element in Project Management," *Project Management Quarterly*, vol. 8, no. 1 (March 1977), p. 118.
25. Erwin S. Stanton, *Reality-Centered People Management* (New York: AMACOM, 1982), p. 27.
26. John D. Borcherding, "Applying Behavioral Research Findings on Construction Projects," *A Decade of Project Management*, John R. Adams and Nicki S. Kirchof, eds. (Drexel Hill, Pa: Project Management Institute, 1981), p. 120.

Index

[Italic page numbers indicate figures and tables.]